CU00949656

About Tryphena
Hardy and his Young Cousin

– NICHOLAS HILLYARD –

[signature]

An environmentally friendly book printed and bound in England by
www.printondemand-worldwide.com

This book is made entirely of chain-of-custody materials

www.fast-print.net/store.php

ABOUT TRYPHENA –
HARDY AND HIS YOUNG COUSIN
Copyright © Nicholas Hillyard 2014

A catalogue record for this book is available from the British Library

ISBN 978-178035-778-2

First published 2014 by
FASTPRINT PUBLISHING
Peterborough, England.

To
John MacAuslan

who made this book
as good as it is

I - INTRODUCTORY

Tryphena Sparks scarcely exists for her own sake. It is her relationship with her cousin Thomas Hardy that gives her a continuing reality. But it is a reality at the mercy of critical revision. As long ago as 1962 Lois Deacon characterised Hardy and Tryphena's relationship as 'an enduring and tragic love-story'. The high tide of this story arrived with *Providence and Mr. Hardy*, the book Terry Coleman helped Lois Deacon to write. For a brief moment Tryphena explained everything. Then the descent of her reputation was vertiginous. Gittings made short work of the cousins' child for which Deacon had argued. He was equally dismissive of Deacon's meteorological research - though this proves to be a rather embarrassing boomerang. A comparison of the two versions of Millgate's big biography shows just how keen he was to put the Sparks genie back in the bottle. He could find no evidence for an engagement between the cousins and felt able to point to only one poem that could definitely be connected with Tryphena - 'Thoughts of Phena' - in which Hardy refers to his cousin as his 'lost prize'. On the evidence of this poem, if on nothing else, some intimate connection between the cousins had to be conceded. But from an 'enduring and tragic love-story' to being 'escorted and mildly courted by her grown-up cousin', as Millgate puts it, the demotion was crushing.

In more recent biographies the pendulum has come to rest between these extremes in what might be called a more modest or reasonable point of view. Such conclusions may seem reasonable just because they are modest. But this does not guarantee that the cousins themselves were reasonable or modest. If mere likelihoods are to be replaced by something more definite new facts are needed. At this late date there is only one place where they are likely to be found. That is in Hardy's own words - or rather, in Hardy's own words in the context of the whole array of facts that biography has so far gathered.

It is perilous to attempt to draw hitherto unheard-of fact out of texts that were never meant to be factual - the poems and the novels. But here Hardy has met us halfway. He frequently introduces a documentary substrate into such texts. There is, for instance, a constant calendar for one particular year of his young manhood which he introduces into the novels over and over again. Once we take this date to Hardy's autobiography some of the more gnomic utterances of *Life* offer remarkable correlations. We can begin to piece together a story which is made certain not merely by the diverse battery of 'documentary' allusions, but by its massive consistency. There is a good deal of detective work to be done before any straightforward narrative becomes possible. It is detective work which carries us inside Hardy's workshop, so that this study inevitably has a dual focus - the story of the cousins and the story of Hardy's authorship. Ultimately this is an advantage, for it becomes clear that authorship itself was an important player in the cousins' drama - and to all appearances a destructive one.

It is perhaps worth outlining Hardy's authorship for some orientation. He began as a poet in his teens. This incipient authorship seems to have been interrupted when he went as an architect's assistant to London, for he speaks of resuming the writing of verses in 1865 when he had been in the capital for three years. In the summer of 1867 he came home to Dorset and early in the next year he had completed his first novel, *The Poor Man and the Lady*. This was never to see the light of day - except in the form of snippets transformed and re-transformed in his later published novels. It was not definitively withdrawn from publishers until the autumn of 1869. Eighteen months later *Desperate Remedies* was published - the novel that begins what I may call the regular series of Wessex Novels which was to end over a quarter of a century later with the publication of *The Well-Beloved* in its re-written form in 1897. As early as Christmas 1890 Hardy had been 'thinking of resuming "the viewless wings of poesy".' His first collection of poems - *Wessex Poems* - was published at the end of 1898 and we may start our investigation at this juncture, for the volume contains 'Thoughts of Phena' - the only point in Hardy's writings where his cousin Tryphena explicitly breaks cover.

II – THE DEATH OF TRYPHENA

Hardy himself connects the poem 'Thoughts of Phena' with his cousin Tryphena's death. In *Life* he includes a journal entry which quotes the first line of the poem, calling it 'a curious instance of sympathetic telepathy. The woman whom I was thinking of - a cousin - was dying at the time, and I quite in ignorance of it.' The journal entry dates to 5 March 1890. Tryphena was to die on the 17th of that month.

Millgate says that the publication of the poem as early as 1898 is evidence that his 'affectionate memories of his dead cousin were unclouded by guilt or self-reproach'. *Tess*, the novel Hardy was writing at the time, suggests a more sombre conclusion. The key to one of its inner meanings is not the journal entry of 5 March 1890, but the one that immediately succeeds it in the text of *Life* - the journal note of 15 March 1890. This note describes Hardy's attendance at a crush at the Jeunes'. Among the guests were the Duchess of Teck 'in black velvet and a few diamonds', her daughter the Princess Mary 'a young woman in skim-milk-blue muslin', Lady Burdett Coutts 'in a head-dress that was a castellated façade of diamonds; she has strongly marked features,' and a 'Mrs. T. and her great eyes in a corner of the rooms, as if washed up by the surging crowd.' The note concludes, 'But these women! If put into rough wrappers in a turnip-field, where would their beauty be?' It is this conclusion that peeps out at us in the episode of Tess's wedding night when Clare decks Tess in his family jewels - 'the beauty of a midnight crush would often cut but a sorry figure if placed inside the field-woman's wrapper upon a monotonous acreage of turnips.' This quotation from the journal is anything but accidental. In the narrative of *Tess* it is a day or two after he has invested Tess with the family diamonds that the sleep-walking Clare wraps her in a sheet 'as in a shroud', lifts her 'with as much respect as one would show to a dead body', carries her across a narrow stream and lays her in a coffin as he chants 'Dead, dead, dead.' Hardy could scarcely be more emphatic. This symbolic death occurs a day or two after the scene in which he directly quotes from the journal note of Lady Jeune's crush on 15 March - just as Tryphena's death had followed that crush by two days on 17 March.

Hardy's quotation of the journal note has every appearance of turning the account of Tess's wedding night and Clare's subsequent sleep-walking into a private memorandum of Tryphena's death. It seems to be something not meant for the reader's attention, but that it was important to Hardy is suggested by the disruption of the manuscript of *Tess*. Laird long ago showed from the foliation of the manuscript that Hardy had specially returned to the account of Tess's wedding night to insert the jewels episode with its quotation of the 15 March journal note. The diamonds, so prominent in that note, now set off the country girl who later, at Flintcomb-Ash, will be 'compelled to don the wrapper of a field-woman'. It is perhaps too simple to say that Hardy has *identified* Tess with Tryphena - but Tryphena is certainly lurking here and her presence may be connected with other details like Tess's intention to become a Pupil Teacher, a career Tryphena Sparks was to pursue with notable success.

In Hardy's very next novel, *The Well-Beloved*, the same journal note of 15 March 1890 bears precisely the same significance. In *Tess* Hardy had quoted directly from the note. In *The Well-Beloved* he repeats the device, but now he feels obliged to hide his traces and be a little less direct. There is the grand society crush when Pierston attends Lady Channelcliffe's reception in the first chapter of the second part of the novel. The journal note of 15 March supplies many of the details of the scene - the black velvet, the diamonds, the muslin. The phrase of the journal note - 'as if washed up by the surging crowd' - may well have suggested the novel's crowd which 'surged upstairs' or the young friend who 'had been brought against [Pierston] by the tide'. But it is the opening paragraph of the succeeding chapter which most intensely reworks the details of the journal note. 'Mrs. T. and her great eyes' becomes Mrs. Pine-Avon's eyes which Pierston 'could not forget...though he remembered nothing of her other facial details.' Lady Burdett Coutts' 'castellated façade of diamonds' and the working women in rough wrappers are conflated in the tiara of the dowager 'who had put ten thousand pounds upon her head to make herself look worse than she would have appeared with the ninepenny muslin cap of a servant woman.'

The autobiographical association remains the same. Within days of Lady Channelcliffe's reception Pierston receives the news of the death of Avice I, the Dorset girl he had loved in his youth.[1] The autobiographical significance of the narrative is amplified by the fact that Pierston now sets off for Portland. *Life* tells us that in the first week of April 1890 Hardy too visited Portland - 'Easter. Sir George Douglas came....next day to

---

[1] In *Tess* the dumbshow of Tryphena's death performed by the sleepwalking Clare occurs precisely two days after the incursion of the 15 March journal note, just as Tryphena's death had occurred two days after the Jeunes' crush on 17 March. In *The Well-Beloved* Pierston receives news of Avice's death a week or so after Lady Channelcliffe's reception - but he receives it by letter so that this week's delay may well reflect the actual date at which Hardy received the news of his cousin's death.

Portland.' - a visit about which we know no more than that the two friends lunched on bread as hard as brickbats. There is therefore a trio of events from his own life which Hardy has introduced into *The Well-Beloved* - the crush at the Jeunes', the death of Tryphena and the Portland visit - each of which is mirrored in the fiction by Lady Channelcliffe's reception, the death of Avice I and Pierston's departure for Portland. In *Tess* Hardy has connected his fictional heroine with Tryphena by his quotation of the journal note of 15 March. In *The Well-Beloved* he has made another such connection - not only by the detailed re-working of the journal note of 15 March, but by surrounding the death of Avice I with precisely those events which had surrounded the death of his cousin Tryphena in March 1890.

The death seems to have had more weight with Hardy than Millgate's airy assessment of 'Thoughts of Phena' suggests. Once the hidden association of Avice I with Hardy's cousin is detected, other filamental connections between the novel and the Tryphena of history begin to suggest themselves. Before her death Avice I is 'bad a long time....She hurt her side with wringing up the large sheets she had to wash.' Tryphena's daughter was to recall her mother's fondness for ducks, that she had 'stooped over to lift a pail of water from the pond, rupturing herself' and that she 'never really recovered from her injury.' More speculatively 'Thoughts of Phena' opens with the words -

> Not a line of her writing have I,
> Not a thread of her hair....

But once Hardy may have had both writing and hair, for the very opening of the novel he began in the year after Tryphena's death - *The Pursuit of the Well-Beloved* - shows the hero burning old love letters and in one bundle, belonging to 'a schoolgirl she', he burns both her letters and her hair. Should these details - and Hardy set them down no more than a year after he had written 'Thoughts of Phena' - be read as a commentary on the poem? Once the hidden references of the novel are brought to light such a connection seems more than likely.

III - THE CHRONOLOGY OF 'THE REVISITATION'

The first Avice is not the only heroine of *The Well-Beloved* who has some hidden connection with Tryphena. This is something that can be established from the poems Hardy wrote at the time of his cousin's death.

Millgate calls 'Thoughts of Phena' 'the one poem that can be confidently associated with Tryphena Sparks,' but I am not alone in considering 'In a Eweleaze Near Weatherbury' to be another. The composition of this poem is dated to the year of her death, 1890. The poem itself is set near Tryphena's birthplace at Puddletown and recalls her vocation in its reference to her 'term as teacher'. These details, taken together, seem to imply that the poem is some sort of elegy. If so, it is an oblique one. But in such a light I suggest the lines

   the little chisel
Of never-napping Time
Defacing wan and grizzel
The blazon of my prime

are an indirect acknowledgement of a physical corruption too horrible for Hardy to express directly. The woman is dead, but the nearest he can come to the reality of this death is the loss of her youthful colour and a slight greying of the hair.

  I could call this merely a hypothesis, but it turns out to be the key to the much more substantial poem 'The Revisitation'. Right away, as Deacon noticed, there is some intimate connection between 'In a Eweleaze' and 'The Revisitation'. In the latter it is now 'Time's transforming chisel' which has tooled too well 'In its rendering of crease where curve was, where was raven, grizzle.' The carrying over of the personified and capitalised 'Time' and the curious 'chisel/grizzel' rhyme from 'In a Eweleaze' is evidently not an accident, for once again we are in the neighbourhood of Puddletown in 1890. No date of composition is given to 'The Revisitation' but its hero twice asserts that his age is fifty years and it was in 1890 that Hardy himself reached fifty. In the topography of the poem this middle-aged hero has walked eastwards from Dorchester to a spot overlooking Puddletown.

  The poem dramatises a nocturnal 'revisitation' to the spot where the speaker had courted a girl twenty years before. Miraculously she appears and the two are re-united until the sun rises and the man wakes and winces at her physical decay and their reconciliation is undone. Puddletown and 1890 - could this fable also have something to do with the death of Tryphena? The details of 'The Revisitation' come into sudden focus as soon as the question is asked.

The whole fable of the poem represents the nocturnal visitation of the woman as a ghost. The lover finds her at midnight - a time which is described as 'this spirit hour' - and when the sun rises she must depart. The details bear out this meaning. The *chiselling* image does not stop at the mild suggestion of lost looks - it is developed to show the woman as 'a thing of skin and bone' with 'a Death's head...not far under'. When the sun rises to lay bare this ruined physique the lover turns 'to take her hanging hand' and is shaken by what appears in her image 'like a spectre' or, as the earliest edition had it, 'like a phantom'. We take it that the 'loosely wrapping vesture' in which she first appeared was already a shroud. What the pitiless morning sun reveals is the reality of death. It is only midnight - 'this spirit-hour' - which holds out the tantalizing illusion that telepathy can 'draw severed souls together'. From this theme we might guess that it is really 'The Revisitation' that gives a comprehensive account of that 'curious instance of sympathetic telepathy' by which the Hardy of *Life* tries to explain the genesis of 'Thoughts of Phena'.

This same Time's Chisel re-appears in the finale of *The Well-Beloved*. Here it is Marcia's features that the cruel morning sun shows ravaged by the 'chisellings' of time. The recurrence of this tell-tale *chiselling* is again no accident. It takes its place in a sequence of details. There is the morning sun, the revelation of ruined beauty, the likening of the woman not now to a 'Death's head...not far under' but to a 'parchment-covered skull'. The prose narrative continues with the lover's involuntary shock, the woman's acknowledgement of her ruined physique, her reproach and his acknowledgement that she has 'A nobler soul than mine' - blow by blow the prose of the novel follows the exact sequence of image and event in the denouement of 'The Revisitation'. It should be no surprise to find this sequence of details from the poem transposed into the novel. *The Well-Beloved* was, after all, begun in the year after Tryphena's death and as we have seen the circumstances surrounding her death were elaborately re-created earlier in the novel's narrative.

With this transposition of 'The Revisitation' into the serial version of *The Well-Beloved* the curtain falls with Pierston's hysterical cry of despair. Even in the revised version of 1897 this moment of horror remains the real goal of the narrative. But surely the poem had already fulfilled a similar function at the conclusion of *Tess*. There the poem's sun-warmed sarsen provides the sun-warmed stone on which Tess lies down as a sacrifice - a motif already hinted at in the poem by naming its heroine Agnette, a lamb. In 'The Revisitation' the woman asks if 'severed souls' can communicate. In the novel Tess asks - 'Angel, do you think we shall meet again after we are dead?' In both the sunrise ends it all.

It may seem that the figure of Tryphena is beginning to appear with alarming frequency at this juncture of Hardy's authorship - that her identity hovers behind the heroine of 'The Revisitation' with its hints of the death of the woman in 1890, that she must therefore be linked with Marcia whose ruined hues are drawn directly from the poem and that she is certainly recalled when the death of the first Avice is so meticulously surrounded by the details which surrounded Tryphena's death. That all three of these heroines are surrogates for Tryphena is something susceptible of mathematical demonstration. The proof makes an interesting excursion into Hardy's symbolic methods.

The hero of 'The Revisitation' twice tells us he is fifty years old - that is, in term's of Hardy's biography, a man of 1890. He also tells us - and again he tells us this twice over in case we should miss the point - that it is 'a lapsing twenty years' since he had parted from the woman 'in a joyless-hued July'. The literal-minded may subtract twenty years from 1890 and conclude that the lovers of the poem parted in the July of 1870. But if Tryphena is the woman of 'The Revisitation' the 'lapsing twenty years' must be adjusted a little. Tryphena died in March 1890 so that the interval between July 1870 and her death, rather than a round twenty, is nearer to nineteen and three quarter years. This pedantic calculation is one Hardy himself is keen to make.

When the first Avice dies Pierston decides to set off for Portland. His friend Somers remonstrates with him - this sudden whim, all for a girl he had last seen a hundred years ago! Pierston replies 'with abstracted literalness' - "No, it was only nineteen." Thus *The Pursuit of the Well-Beloved* in 1892. But the calculation was not quite precise enough. When Hardy rewrote the novel in 1897 he altered Pierston's literal and abstracted reply to - "No - it was only nineteen and three quarters." It is 'The Revisitation' which explains the extraordinary literalness of this emendation. 'The Revisitation' fits like the perfect key with its hint that Hardy last saw his cousin in July 1870, precisely nineteen and three-quarter years before her death!

This little calculation makes a number of things clear. It shows with crystal clarity that 'The Revisitation' is indeed an elegy. It confirms the connection between the first Avice and Tryphena and it shows that the heroine of 'The Revisitation' - and therefore Marcia too - are equally surrogates for Hardy's dead cousin. But this calculation has also told us something entirely unexpected - that the July of the lovers' parting in 'The Revisitation' only makes sense of the revision in *The Well-Beloved* because it is a real date of history. It shows that Hardy and his cousin last saw each other in July 1870. The finding puts paid to Gittings' speculation that Tryphena had gone home to Dorset in this summer and that Hardy's departure from London to Cornwall was determined by her return to London for her new term at the Training College in Stockwell. He has got these events pretty well back to front. *Life* records Hardy being in London from the spring through until August. It therefore seems that his last meeting with his cousin in the July must have been in the capital.

There is a behind-the-scenes consistency here which enables us to recover this hitherto unknown fact of Hardy's biography. The consistency is highly deliberate. Hardy has not pulled his precise nineteen-and-three-quarter year emendation out of thin air. I shall be looking for similar kinds of consistency which go beyond any literary demands and therefore require an explanation beyond the purely literary. A sense of security in such a pragmatic method may be gained by staying for the moment on our newly discovered territory, for it seems that the nineteen-and-three-quarter year interval between Hardy's parting from Tryphena and her death is the template on which the whole structure of *The Well-Beloved* is built up.

IV - THE NINETEEN-AND-THREE-QUARTER YEAR TEMPLATE

'A Young Man of Twenty', 'A Young Man of Forty', 'A Young Man of Sixty' - each part of *The Well-Beloved* is a cycle of twenty or so years and the first of them, from twenty to forty, is measured explicitly on the interval between the lover's parting and the death of Avice the First - or, for the private Hardy musing on his own creation, the interval between July 1870 when he last saw Tryphena and the March 1890 of her death. The death of Avice the First ushers in a new cycle. But here Hardy has contrived a scene beside the grave of this first Avice Caro to suggest that her successor is not so much a daughter who looks extraordinarily like her mother as the *same* Avice reborn. Pierston is made to see the new Avice as the original 'Avice Caro herself, bending over and then withdrawing from her grave in the light of the moon,' or, as the 1892 serial version even more succinctly puts it, 'Avice Caro herself, standing beside her own grave.' Pierston wrestles with the 'impossibility' that this can be the first Avice who could 'not now look the same as she had appeared nineteen or twenty years ago.' But this 'dream-fancy' that the dead woman is restored just as she had been when her lover last saw her is, of course, the basis of the whole fable of 'The Revisitation'. Agnette says "It is *just* as ere we parted!" - an illusion maintained until the cruel rising of the morning sun.

When the third Avice appears at the beginning of the next twenty year cycle it is as 'the very she, in all essential particulars, and with an intensification of general charm, who had kissed him forty years before.' In the background she is still somehow the *same* Tryphena too. Great play is made of lending this third Avice a textbook from which Hardy himself had learned French in the mid 1860s. Millgate records the family tradition about Tryphena that Hardy 'is said to have undertaken to teach her French.' With the appearance of Avice III Hardy slightly diversifies the symmetry of the story, but the older Avice - now Avice the Second - is not long in dying. Her death is dictated by the new twenty year leap from parting to death. The whole novel is only an extended re-enactment of the fable of 'The Revisitation' where, after a twenty year absence, the beloved appears once more in her original youthfulness at the moment of her death.[2]

---

[2] See section XXIX below for the motif of the photograph which, like a neatly-fitting jigsaw piece, simultaneously reminds Pierston of both Avice as a young woman and the young woman Marcia had been.

It is now clear why Hardy placed his paraphrase of 'The Revisitation' at the close of the novel. It expresses the *realisation* of death and in the serial version the narrative disintegrated at this point with Pierston's hysterical cry, 'O - no, no! I - I - it is too, too droll - this ending to my would-be romantic history!' In *Tess* too the poem appears as the goal or 'fulfilment' of the narrative - a symbolic death on the stone of sacrifice which endorses the emphasis I have laid on the deathly hints of 'The Revisitation' itself. But Tryphena conditions the structuring of *The Well-Beloved* in a far more thoroughgoing way than she does in *Tess*.

The nineteen and three-quarter year template, measured from the moment Hardy last saw his cousin to her death in 1890, is not a complete explanation of the structure of *The Well-Beloved*. There is an extraordinary and wholly accidental symmetry without which Hardy could not have made his cyclic structure mirror the life of the girl for whom the novel is beginning to appear to be some sort of elaborate mausoleum. Tryphena was born in March 1851, so at her parting from Hardy in July 1870 she was nineteen. The span from July 1870 to her death in March 1890 was also one of nineteen years. It is this wholly accidental symmetry that the novel's structure takes advantage of by allowing the new Avice to grow to precisely the age of the dead Avice when the hero had known her twenty - or nineteen and three quarter - years before. Avice II is 'Going in nineteen' and the narrative tells us 'It was about the age of her double, Avice the First,' when she and Pierston had strolled over the cliffs of Portland in the romance of the novel's

Part First. When added together nineteen and nineteen-and-three-quarters would give the first Avice an age of thirty-eight at her death. Tryphena was to die a few days short of her thirty-ninth birthday.

In the novel - just as with the fable of 'The Revisitation' - it is the superimposition of the nineteen year old girl on a Death's Head which chastens Pierston - or Hardy the poet. The death of Avice the First nineteen years after the hero had last seen her coincides with the appearance of the nineteen-year-old Avice the Second who looks exactly like the first Avice and is initially seen standing beside her grave as though she had just emerged from it. At the death of Avice II the third Avice is once more a girl of this age and once again this third Avice is 'the very she, in all essential particulars...who had kissed him forty years before.' The Avices are the same over and over again. In terms of Hardy's psychology we may speculate that a new Avice must instantly fill up the place of the dead Avice because of that horror of physical decay which hovers about 'In a Eweleaze' and more explicitly 'The Revisitation' - a theme emphatically repeated in the finale of *The Well-Beloved* with its parchment-covered skull and its grim quotation from Isaiah - 'Instead of sweet smell there shall be stink, and there shall be burning instead of beauty.' Youth and the reality of death make an extraordinarily stark confrontation. But for Hardy, since he had last seen his dead cousin as a young woman of nineteen, there was nothing to hold them apart.

The careful connection of the first Avice - and, indeed, of Marcia - with his cousin and the cyclic structure of the book with its nineteen and three-quarter year template are inseparable parts of a single conception in which Hardy has made of *The Well-Beloved* in both detail and over-arching form a veritable monument to the dead Tryphena Sparks. Those little moments of identification like the deployment of the 15 March journal note or the French studies of Avice III have their place in a narrative whose whole shape is generated by the historical Tryphena. It now seems probable that the burning of a schoolgirl's letters and hair in the original opening of the serial version is the explanation of why the Hardy of 'Thoughts of Phena' had not a line of his cousin's writing, not a thread of her hair. We may surmise that he had burned these relics some time before 1890.

V - A YOUNG MAN OF 'NEARLY FIFTY'

Enough of *The Well-Beloved*! Or almost enough. The death of Tryphena has given us the clue by which we can make an entry into the labyrinth of the novel's construction - one further detail makes of *The Well-Beloved* a bridge to the reconstruction of Hardy's whole affair with his young cousin. The heroine is a girl who must always be reincarnated in her nineteenth year, but the artist hero who is her lover marks time in a rather different way. A Young Man of Twenty! A Young Man of Forty! A Young Man of Sixty! Hardy flings the awful anomaly of what Pierston is in our faces in the very titles to the three parts of the novel. But the unnatural longevity of this 'Young Man' comes to an end. The hero suddenly ages.

·

Both versions of *The Well-Beloved* agree on this demise. In the 1892 version Pierston says that due to his illness he has 'become an old man during the last month'. In the 1897 version the theme is made more emphatic - 'numbering in years but two-and-sixty, he might have passed for seventy-five.' Of this sudden ageing Pierston says, 'Thank Heaven I am old at last. The curse is removed.' The sense of release only draws attention to the weirdness of Pierston's longevity as a 'young man'. But the 'young man' of curious longevity appears elsewhere in Hardy's writing and quite outside the realm of fiction.

In *Life* - in connection with 'his lateness of development in virility' - Hardy remarks 'that he was a child till he was sixteen, a youth till he was five-and-twenty, and a young man till he was nearly fifty.' Here once more is the *young man* of strange longevity. But the ages given in this little aside are not round numbers - least of all the phrase 'nearly fifty'. In *The Pursuit of the Well-Beloved* Pierston dramatically ceases to be a young man in the course of the month's illness contracted at the funeral of the second Avice. We must now take this funeral to be a reference to the death of a Tryphena who had made her cyclic appearance as Avice II when she was seen withdrawing from the grave of that first Avice whom Hardy had so carefully linked with his cousin in the circumstances surrounding her death. The course of Pierston's illness is also punctuated by the appearance of the aged Marcia bringing with her that incursion of material from 'The Revisitation' - one of Hardy's earliest poetic responses to the death of his cousin - so that the two heroines doubly connect the illness through which Pierston suddenly ceases to be a young man with Tryphena's death. The hint is a perfect match with what Hardy tells us in his autobiography.

In the March 1890 when Tryphena died Hardy was just two and a half months short of his fiftieth birthday, so that when he says in *Life* that he ceased to be a young man when he was 'nearly fifty' this dating flawlessly mirrors the implication of *The Well-Beloved* where the illness by which Pierston ceases to be a young man is bracketed by the deaths of two heroines identified with Tryphena. Hardy - and who can stop him? - seems to cross the frontier between fiction and reality with the greatest of ease. He has used his fiction to record the fact that it was Tryphena's death which put an end to the protracted existence of both his artist hero and himself as a *young man*. In this 'nearly fifty' of the autobiography Hardy is evidently applying just the same sort of 'abstracted literalness' in matters of chronology as his hero Pierston.

The consistencies between novel and autobiography allow us to begin to peer into the meaning of Hardy's life as he himself conceived it. There is something deliberately cryptic in his account of 'his lateness of development in virility' in *Life*, but it now seems that this strange suspension of continuing to be a young man deep into middle age is bound up with Hardy's relationship with Tryphena Sparks. When she dies Hardy ceases to be a young man. As long as she was alive his young manhood could somehow be prolonged.

VI - THE 1865 CALENDAR

We have a solution for the 'nearly fifty' of Hardy's gnomic commentary on 'his lateness of development in virility'. But how about the 'five-and-twenty' at which Hardy first became a young man? Can this too have anything to do with Tryphena? The question might be put another way. Why, of all the young women Hardy may have known, should it be precisely Tryphena who put an end to his young manhood - unless she had also had something to do with her cousin becoming a 'young man' in the first place?

This question can be left hanging in the air. First of all it can be shown that there is rather interesting evidence about the year in which Hardy became a young man at the age of twenty-five. His twenty-fifth birthday fell at the beginning of June 1865. 1865 is a year over which Gittings, with excellent intuition, hovered tantalisingly. Its importance can be underlined by a brief collection of the calendars concealed in the narratives of various novels. I have put the publication dates of the relevant novels in brackets so that we can see how over time Hardy developed ever more arcane ways of introducing his constant calendar.

In the chapter headings of *Desperate Remedies* (1871) we soon reach an explicit date in 1863 and the subsequent headings consist of nothing but a series of indications of months or precise time-spans. When all these are added together they bring us to the heart of the novel - Manston's courtship of Cytherea - in the summer of 1865.

In *A Pair of Blue Eyes* (1873) the first volume edition attached a date of '1864' to the architect's correspondence about the restoration of the church - though this was later removed - so that Knight's subsequent courtship of Elfride also falls in the summer of 1865. The fragmentary manuscript of the novel gives further evidence that the novel's calendar was based on this year.

In *The Return of the Native* (1878) the calendar is more artfully concealed. Days of the week coincide with dates of the month to make an exact match with the calendar of 1865 so that the thirty-first of August falls emphatically on a Thursday as it did in that year and the dates of 5 November and Boxing Day in the previous year fall on the appropriate days of the week specified by the narrative for late 1864. The 1865 of this calendar is confirmed in various ways - by the exceptional summer weather of the historical 1865 which is faithfully depicted in the August weather in which Mrs. Yeobright dies and by Hardy's advice about Clym Yeobright in a letter to his illustrator that 'A thoughtful young man of 25 is all that can be shown', though the hero's precise age is nowhere given in the text of the novel. This looks suspiciously like an autobiographical assumption that because Hardy was twenty-five in 1865 Clym must also have been twenty-five. This summer of 1865 sees the courtship of Clym and Eustacia.

In *An Indiscretion in the Life of an Heiress* (1878) Hardy makes his hero an author. The appearance of Egbert Mayne's book is an elaborately circumstantial reference to the publication of *Desperate Remedies*. The two-word title of the book is indicating by two long dashes, it is published anonymously and it receives three favourable reviews from weighty literary periodicals of the day. All these details faithfully reflect what *Life* has to say about the publication of *Desperate Remedies*. Hardy seems to be using the 1871 publication of *Desperate Remedies* as a date-peg, for with a precise time-span he calculates back from the appearance of Mayne's book to the date of the hero and heroine's romance on no fewer than six occasions. The time spans consistently take us back to the summer of 1865 as the date of the romance. After the publication of the book which is evidently *Desperate Remedies* the hero, Egbert Mayne, suffers a reaction - having lost his lady 'he was now a man who had no further motive in moving on.'

Now the device that Hardy uses in *An Indiscretion* has been brought into focus we can see that he re-used it in *The Well-Beloved* (1892-7). Here the publication of *Desperate Remedies* seems to be glossed as Pierston becoming A.R.A. The suspicion that becoming A.R.A. means Hardy's first public appearance as a novelist is confirmed at the end of *The Well-Beloved* - the novel which in its thorough-going revision is really Hardy's last. It is only now, in this 1897 version, that Hardy perfects a Prospero-like farewell to novel-writing by noting that his artist hero's name 'figured on the retired list of Academicians'. But what seems to be Hardy's allusion to the first appearance of *Desperate Remedies* is attended by just the same sensations of pointlessness which Mayne had experienced at the much more explicit reference to the publication of *Desperate*

Remedies in *An Indiscretion* - 'for want of a domestic centre, round which honours might crystallize, they dispersed in impalpable vapour'. Again Hardy seems to be using the reference as a date-peg for he makes just the same retrospective calculation that he had made in *An Indiscretion* to date the courtship of Pierston and Avice I to the summer of 1865.[3]

From the undisguised assertion of *Desperate Remedies* or *A Pair of Blue Eyes* to the arcane methods of *The Return of the Native*, *An Indiscretion* and *The Well-Beloved* Hardy's allusions to a calendar of 1865 betray an air of progressive caution. The elaborate nature of the disguises he came to invent suggests that the date itself was both of vital importance to him and something in the nature of a secret. The importance is explicit in *Life*. Here Hardy calls 'his lateness of development in virility', to which his gnomic chronology is attached, 'a clue to much of his character and action throughout his life'. The element of secrecy is also becoming clearer

---

[3] Pierston makes his first appearance as 'A Young Man of Twenty'. If this is in an autobiographical 1865 we must add five years since Hardy was twenty-five in 1865. So when we are told of 'the productive interval which followed the first years of Marcia's departure, when he was drifting along from five-and-twenty' we must add five years to this 'five-and-twenty' to bring it up to the real life age of thirty - which was Hardy's age when *Desperate Remedies* was published. This interpretation is supported by the parallel passage of the 1892 version of the novel where 'four years of common residence' with Marcia and an unspecified period of separation intervene between the opening Portland scene and Pierston's becoming A.R.A. The calculation is confirmed at the denouement of the tale where, with the incursion of material from 'The Revisitation', Marcia admits that 'the moth eats the garment somewhat in five-and-thirty years' - i.e. since Pierston had last seen her. The narrative opened forty years before. This thirty-five years back recalls the 1870 in which Hardy last saw Tryphena. The forty years back at which the novel opens is therefore 1865.

now we have unravelled at least one part of the riddling chronology - the 'nearly fifty' at which Hardy ceased to be a young man, which is his oblique reference to the death of his cousin Tryphena. We can begin to imagine both why this 1865 calendar is so often repeated and why it is concealed.

The list is not exhaustive. The meteorology of the historical summer of 1865 was exceptional. The *Times* stated that it had been the hottest May since records began and this weather continued unabated into the second week of October. At the beginning of August 1865 the *Dorset County Chronicle* spoke of 'the heat and glory of an Italian summer' and in September could claim that 'this summer of glorious splendour has scarcely yet left us'. This would seem to be the 'Thermidorean' weather of *Tess*, a speculation confirmed by the little detail of cabbage and rhubarb leaves 'hanging in the sun like half closed umbrellas.' This is a verbatim parallel with the words describing the hollyhock leaves which 'hung like half-closed umbrellas' in the account of the blazing summer of *The Return of the Native* which is dated to 1865 by that novel's calendar.

Rutland was the first to pay attention to such verbal parallelisms or *doublets* as he called them. From their frequency in *An Indiscretion* - the novella so closely connected with *The Poor Man* - he argued that these doublets occur because Hardy had lifted the same text from that abandoned first novel on more than one occasion. Getting on for a score of such passages can be isolated. At first sight one might think they only crop up as verbatim doublets because Hardy's record of just what he had lifted from the suppressed manuscript was rather inefficient. Such carelessness may account for many of them, but there are also examples where a particular passage has been sedulously reworked over and over again. That such multiple re-usings were highly conscious can be seen from the care with which Hardy begins to disguise and vary the repetitions. The fact that he made such a thematic use of the suppressed novel seriously undermines the conventional view set afoot by Weber that he used up the text of *The Poor Man* in economic fashion by simply parcelling it out among his earlier novels.[4] The presence of the doublets can still be detected as late as *Tess* and *The Well-Beloved*. Where a particular passage is used repeatedly such doublets seem to preserve some moment of special importance in the narrative of the suppressed novel.

The most striking of these doublets, as we shall see, is one describing gnats dancing in a sunset which in its fullest form occurs in both *The Return of the Native* and in *Desperate Remedies*. Both these novels agree in assigning the description of the sunset gnats to the summer of 1865, suggesting that *The Poor Man* from which the passage originally came also had a calendar for 1865. The suggestion is backed up by those leaves hanging 'like half-closed umbrellas'. In *The Return of the Native* this doublet is part of the elaborate description of an exceptional summer to which the novel's calendar

---

[4] The theory overlooks the difficulty that *The Poor Man* was told in the first person - a fact which would have posed a considerable barrier to any scissors and paste work with the original. We only have to think of Hardy's complaints as an experienced novelist about the 're-membering' of *Tess* after its *dis*memberment - a comparatively simple task.

gives the date 1865. The Thermidorean weather of *Tess* shows not only the leaves hanging like half-closed umbrellas, but a number of other verbatim parallels shared with the description of the summer 1865 in which Yeobright courts Eustacia in *The Return of the Native*. The agreement of the calendars of the novels in which these descriptions occur and the meteorological conditions of the historical 1865 point to the summer of 1865 as the date at which the romance of *The Poor Man* was set. When we see that *A Laodicean* also opens in a hot summer where gnats are seen dancing in the sunset and in which the hero is twenty-five it seems we are once more in a familiar web of consistencies.

From this standpoint it looks as if Gittings's rough handling of Lois Deacon's meteorological 'research' is an embarrassing boomerang. True, her attribution of 'a year with a splendid Indian summer' to 1867 is scarcely supported by the weather records. But her belief, encouraged by her reading of *Tess*, that Hardy and his cousin became lovers in such a summer with its 'long, hot autumn' could have some basis in fact after all - if that summer was the summer of 1865.

VII - THE MAIDEN OF 1865

Hardy returns to this calendar of 1865 repeatedly. It seems that it has a significance he cannot escape. In the novels it is always the date of an affair and this surely provides a very simple explanation of why Hardy's clue in his autobiography speaks of *becoming a young man* at this time. After all, he makes that claim in the context of 'his lateness of development in virility' - a phrase which points us in the direction of an affair and therefore, it seems, an affair of his twenty-fifth year. The obsessive repetition of the calendar suggests that this was an affair that left ineradicable marks on him. But it is not necessary to rely on the consistency of the novels with the *Life* to date such an affair. Hardy has left the clearest contemporary evidence in the verse he wrote at the time.

In *Life* Hardy tells us that 1865 was the first year in which he began to write poetry again since his move to London as an architect's assistant. At least thirty-five poems survive from the period 1865-7 - a burst of activity brought to an end by the start of work on *The Poor Man* and Hardy's return home to Dorset. These poems were dominated by the figure of a woman - or girl - whom Hardy calls a 'maid' or 'maiden'. This is the title she is given as the heroine of the 'She, to Him' sonnets, of four other sonnets related to them, of 'The Two Men', 'The Musing Maiden', 'Her Definition', 'The Unplanted Primrose' and also, if it is accepted as a poem of 1867, 'The Temporary the All'. This tally amounts to over a third of the surviving poems of 1865-7, but the proportion was certainly larger since Hardy describes the four surviving 'She, To Him' sonnets as 'part of a much larger number which perished'. Had he not destroyed the bulk of his sonnet cycle the *maiden* would have publicly dominated this early phase of his poetry, presenting herself as an irresistible candidate for the circumstances which lie behind Hardy's becoming a young man at the age of twenty-five.

The fact that Hardy refers to his cousin in 'Thoughts of Phena' as 'that maiden of yore' may be no more than coincidence. 'Maiden' is a word he might have applied to a multiplicity of young women or girls. But he is thinking of a single one in the poems of 1865-7. In 'She, to Him' I the word is used as a title with appropriate capitals as 'Maiden Fair and Free'. Not only are almost all the poems of 1865-7 in which the word is used unified by the failure of an affair and an implication of the lover's guilt but Hardy seems to have the distinct feeling that he had used the title *maiden* with revealing frequency. So he substituted the word 'jade' for 'maid' in 'She, to Him' II, though the manuscript and the prosing of the poem in *Desperate Remedies* show that 'maid' was the original reading.[5] And when he prepared 'The Unplanted Primrose' for publication - though the poem was finally omitted from *Winter Words* - the manuscript shows that he cancelled the word 'maiden' and obliged himself to find the lamest of substitutes to fill out of the rhythm of the line.

It seems that the first flush of this affair with a maiden must be placed some time between 1865 and the 1866 in which the 'She, to Him' sonnets were composed - sonnets which already look back guiltily on the failure of the affair. This is also the implication of

---

[5] The manuscript notes 'Prosed in "Desperate Remedies"' - where a prose rendering of the sonnet occurs. Such prosings were presumably lifted from *The Poor Man* for Hardy originally called that novel a story 'Containing some original verses' - an indication he dropped while working on the book. Presumably the suppression of these original verses left narrative blanks which would have to have been bridged by prose versions of the poems which had disappeared.

that unpublished poem 'The Unplanted Primrose'. Hardy dates it '1865-67', its action takes place in the summer and refers to a more promising phase of its maiden's romance 'a year before'. Given that the 'She, to Him' sonnets of 1866 show the maiden's romance as one that had already failed, the 'summer before' of 'The Unplanted Primrose' would seem to be that of 1865.

There are one or two hints to be gathered about this maiden. In 'From Her in the Country' she calls herself a 'rural maid' and in 'The Unplanted Primrose' there is a clear evocation of the cottage garden at Bockhampton, a spot from which the maiden lives distant 'a little mile'. So she was a Dorset girl. But this raises a slight difficulty. In the summer of 1865 Hardy was ostensibly not in Dorset but in London.

VIII - ADJUSTING THE OFFICIAL RECORD

In this one respect the summer of 1865 seems a little problematic as the date for an affair like the one implied by the poems of 1865-7 or, indeed, like any of those intense country courtships outlined in the novels at a calendar of 1865. Hardy gives no hint that he was not working as an architect's assistant in London throughout this year. An affair might have been conducted by week-end visits and the rest have been achieved by correspondence - or a novelist's imagination. But could this affair - which, from the date of the 'She, to Him' sonnets onwards, seems to have left so deep a mark on Hardy - have been a casual thing? And if it was not a casual thing could it really have been conducted at a distance? If we apply a little 'abstracted literalness' of our own to the problem of getting Hardy to Dorset for a serious affair in the summer of 1865 the results are rather startling.

In *Life* Hardy describes an illness which drove him from his work in London as architect's assistant in 'Summer 1867' - at least, that is the heading he gives this section of his autobiography. Subsequent biographers have followed Hardy's lead with unquestioning docility. But there is something that does not ring true about the account. An implication of crisis is clearly evident. Hardy describes his alarming symptoms in detail, he notes their advance 'month by month', friends in Dorset are 'shocked at the pallor which sheeted a countenance formerly ruddy with health', 'on sitting down to begin drawing in the morning he had scarcely physical power left him to hold the pencil and square.' His employer, Blomfield, suggests that he goes home 'to regain vigour', but that he should return to London 'by the following October at latest'. The stipulation surely implies that he would keep Hardy's job open until then. Since Hardy left London 'at the latter part of July' Blomfield must have envisaged a recuperative holiday of at least nine weeks. This seems an objective measure of the seriousness of Hardy's condition. The advance of the debility 'month by month' until Hardy could scarcely hold a pencil and square describes a crisis that came to a head by the late July when Hardy went home to Bockhampton.

But something very different is going on as well. Hardy sedately remarks that Blomfield 'must have been inconvenienced' by his illness. But the typescript of *Life* shows that this aside originally continued - 'through his plans and elevations not getting finished as promptly as before'. The admission explains why Blomfield advised his young assistant to have a complete break - Hardy had evidently reached a state in which he could not hold down his job. But in the narrative of *Life* Hardy has to tone down the severity of his illness - there is no other way to give verisimilitude to the claim that despite being forced to leave Blomfield's office by this illness he blithely recommended himself to his old Dorchester boss Hicks to continue architectural work with no break at all. Hardy himself seems to realise the dilemma - he calls the move an 'experiment' and crosses out the admission that he was not getting his plans and elevations finished on time. All of a sudden the crisis is not really a crisis and that there was in fact no crisis of the kind Hardy describes in the summer of 1867 is made clear enough by the one extant contemporary document with a bearing on the matter.

In the Dorset County Museum there is a letter from Hardy's friend Horace Moule dated June 1867. It is a breezy letter in which Moule won't try very hard 'to affect a meeting in Town, spite of Patti and Titiens'. The reason for this cheerful negligence lies in the first line of the letter which is the whole occasion of Moule's note - 'I am delighted to hear of yr intended move in our direction.'[6] The story of a crisis departure

---

[6] The untroubled tone makes makes an instructive contrast with a reminiscence of Henry Moule, Horace's brother, which Hardy recalls in the preface he wrote for Henry Moule's *Dorchester Antiquities* - 'But a continuous residence in London of several years having begun to tell upon my health I determined to go into the country for a time. He heard of my plan, and wrote to me suggesting estate-management as a change of

from London in late July must go out of the window. Clearly Hardy had laid plans to leave London at least as early as June. We can make a very plausible guess at his motivation for this plan - a guess which further exposes the shakiness of the 'Summer 1867' narrative in *Life*.

Hardy tells us he returned to the country at the end of July 1867, that he resumed verse 'awhile' then laid it aside for the prose of *The Poor Man and the Lady* which he wrote 'in the intervals of his attendances at Mr. Hicks's drawing-office' and finished by mid-January 1868. The assertion is not really believable. *The Poor Man* was Hardy's first novel and it was to be a three-volume one. Yet the time-table Hardy gives himself - scarcely five months, given his resumption of verse, and not even taking into account his work for Hicks - is much briefer than the time it took him to write any of the other early novels for which we have exact dates of composition. The timetable takes no account of Hardy's severe debility, part of which he attributes to the mind-work of 'reading incessantly'. Not only this, but Hardy explicitly recalled to his friend Gosse that 'It took him a long time to finish, and now and then he could not get the story to move; it 'stuck'.'

We may feel that Hardy's recollection of the real course of events was clear enough for him to feel the implausibility of the story he is telling in *Life*. In its narrative a note of 16 January 1868 reminds him that 'he began to make a fair copy of the projected story, so

---

occupation, which would give me plenty of air.' This, no doubt, was the Moules' response to Hardy's debility in 1865. Aeneas Manston arrives in Dorset as Land Steward in the summer 1865 of *Desperate Remedies*.

that all of it must have been written out roughly during the preceding five months.' This 'must have been' seems suspiciously circumstantial. Hardy does not quote the note of 16 January, but he does reproduce that of 9 June. This simply says, 'Finished copying MS.' with no hint that he had also been rewriting his novel.[7] We shall, I think, soon see that the logic of these difficulties is simply this - Hardy had begun work on *The Poor Man* much earlier than he says, that by at least as early as June 1867 he had planned to return home to complete the novel and that this is why he took on part-time work with Hicks. Such an arrangement - starting a book away from home and returning to Bockhampton to complete it - was to be Hardy's routine with each of the novels he wrote up to the time of his marriage to Emma Gifford.

The difficulties of Hardy's account of the writing of *The Poor Man* are of a piece with the difficulties of believing that he could instantly have recommended himself to Hicks in the throes of the crisis which forced him to leave Blomfield's office. I have followed the logic of Horace Moule's letter in suggesting that the severe illness which drove Hardy from London does

---

[7] Millgate tries to save the appearances by referring to George Sharpe's 21 January 1868 letter of medical suggestions as evidence that the fair-copying 'involved expansion as well as revision'. But looked at closely Sharpe's tell-tale phrase in connection with the temporary blindness 'as you suggest' and the concession that 'Haemorrage...is less prosaically common than inflammation would be for your purpose' suggest that Hardy may already have had the medical details clear in his mind and had merely written to Sharpe for a second opinion. Sharpe's apology for his very long delay in writing suggest a date for Hardy's enquiries well before the start of fair-copying on 16 January at which the denouement of the tale with the death of the Lady could already have been worked out.

not belong to 1867 at all. If so, we are looking for an alternative date. The year 1865 recommends itself with an extraordinary consistency. That most visible symptom of Hardy's illness - 'the pallor which sheeted a countenance formerly ruddy with health' - is already in evidence in two poems of 1866. In 'Her Dilemma' the hero is 'So wan and worn that he could scarcely stand'. The qualification 'scarcely' has occurred before - Hardy, in addition to his shocking pallor, had '*scarcely* physical power left him to hold the pencil and square'. 'The Two Men', also of 1866, has the look of an allegory constructed around a young man's worldly failure due to an illness which has the same symptoms and causes as those given in *Life* under the heading 'Summer 1867' - the 'features wan', the weakness and the over-studious habits are all here. For Hardy's incapacitating illness we seem, on the evidence of his dating of these two poems, to be looking to a date of 1866 or earlier.

There can be no doubt that the illness described in *Life* is the one which is given to the young architect Owen Graye in *Desperate Remedies*. Owen, like Hardy, is an architect's assistant, employed not by Mr. Blomfield but by a Mr. Gradfield. He suffers from a progressive, undiagnosed debility accompanied by a striking pallor - when his sister visits him she finds him 'startlingly thin and pale.' The fact that Owen is reduced to working at his drawing-board sitting down preserves Hardy's own recollection that he had 'scarcely physical power left him to hold the pencil and square'. The crisis of Owen's illness - like Hardy's - is set precisely in late July. But according to the novel's explicit calendar this is not in the late July of 1867 but at the end of July 1865.

In the summer 1865 of the calendar of *The Return of the Native* we learn that the 'paleness of face' which Clym had brought from Paris is now 'less perceptible' than when he returned at Christmas - 'the healthful and energetic sturdiness which was his by nature having partially recovered its original proportions.' This is an authorial gaffe. The implication of the words *partially recovered* is clearly that Clym has been gravely ill, though - extraordinarily - this is a fact entirely unknown to the rest of the narrative. Has Hardy been decoyed into giving Clym such an illness because he himself was seriously ill in the 1865 of the novel's calendar?[8] It looks to be precisely another of those

---

[8] Clym's illness appears to be repeated from that of Will Strong - hero of *The Poor Man*. In January 1868 Hardy's uncle, George Brereton Sharpe, writes 'a loss of sight...might result as you suggest - from continued study late at night of small print or Greek characters - feeble light would aid - and debilitating causes would increase the tendency to temporary blindness.' Hardy's suggestion seems a blue-print for Clym's affliction in the summer 1865 of *The Return of the Native*. In the 'Summer 1867' of *Life* Hardy attributes his debility in part to late night reading, shutting himself up in his lodgings 'every evening from six to twelve reading incessantly.' That this is a reminiscence of a year prior to 1867 is clear from stanzas 5-7 of the 1866 poem 'The Two Men' - a vignette which might be illustrated by the 2 June 1865 journal note which describes Hardy reading until half past twelve. Under the years 1872-3 in *Life* Hardy recalls Moule's anxiety 'supposing anything were to happen to his [Hardy's] eyes from the fine architectural drawing' and the 'strange coincidence' that shortly afterwards he saw 'for the first time in his life, what seemed like floating specks on the white drawing-paper'. The assertion of 'strange coincidence' looks like a characteristic example of Hardy's naivety. When we note in *An Indiscretion* that among the symptoms of Farmer Broadford's July 1865 debility is 'dimness of sight' we may be tempted to conclude that Will Strong of *The Poor Man* was given some eye-complaint because Hardy himself had suffered something of the kind in summer 1865. Intriguingly, in a letter of

unconscious assumptions like Hardy's attribution of the age of twenty-five to Clym in his letter to his illustrator - because he himself had been twenty-five in the 1865 of the novel's covert chronology. Clym has, of course, thrown up his work in a big city and come home.

Then there is the opening of *A Laodicean* - young George Somerset has just thrown up his job as architect's assistant in London and come to the country. Again he is twenty-five. Something more than co-incidence is going on here. We are told that it is August when the 'pale face' of the townsman is seen in the country. Somerset is a townsman who has just come to the country and so is, by implication, a young man who also has a pale face. Though we are not told that he is ill - just as we were not told that Clym was ill - it is curious how this little complex of chronology, pallor and loss of employment persists.

The consistency of these references in the fictions and the consistency of the fictions with the hints of those 1866 poems 'Her Dilemma' and 'The Two Men' - not least the tell-tale pallor common to them all - justify detaching the story of Hardy's severe illness from the narrative of 'Summer 1867' and placing it in its proper context of July 1865.[9] The reconstruction which Moule's letter invites is now plain sailing - that

---

March 1902, he writes, 'I, too, suffer in one of my eyes sometimes...It comes on in hot weather in London...' The spring of 1865 when Hardy was in London was the hottest on record.

[9] This is precisely what we are invited to do by *Life's* egregious misplacing of the riddling note of 'End of Dec. 1865.' at the close of the section entitled 'Summer 1867'.

Hardy cooly planned his return to Bockhampton in the summer of 1867 not because he was ill but because he had embarked on the writing of *The Poor Man*. Once we disencumber the story of 1867 of a severe illness not only does the time-span for the writing of *The Poor Man* become intelligible - not forgetting the fact that Hardy found the composition slow going - but so too does his instant recommendation of himself to Hicks. This part-time work in Dorchester was no doubt a minimum condition to placate the parents under whose roof he was now pursuing a literary venture of very doubtful practicality.[10] The contradictions of *Life's* narrative of Summer 1867 vanish once they are met by the evidence of the dates Hardy gives to 'Her Dilemma' and 'The Two Men', of the consistent hints of the 1865 calendars of the novels and by Horace Moule's contemporary letter.

Once we take up the suggestion of the novels' calendars and re-assign Hardy's illness to the summer of 1865 other details fall into place. There is now an explanation of how Hardy could be present in Dorset - perhaps for a good part of the nine weeks recommended by Blomfield - for that affair which the calendars of the novels refer over and over again to the summer of 1865. Or - if this is too fictive - for that affair which lies behind the poems for the Maiden which were written between 1865 and 1867.

---

[10] At the opening of *A Laodicean* George Somerset is given 'a severe hint from his father that unless he went on with his legitimate profession he might have to look elsewhere than at home for an allowance.' At Clym's return from the great city Mrs. Yeobright complains, 'After all the trouble that has been taken to give you a start, and when there is nothing to do but to keep straight on towards affluence.'

Speaking of the illness which drove Hardy from London Millgate preserves what seems ultimately to have been Hardy's own recollection that he had 'had to face the scorn of friends and neighbours who interpreted his retreat to Bockhampton as a clear sign that he had been defeated in his attempt to make his way in the larger world'. We may set the wording of this admission beside a journal note that Hardy added to the typescript of *Life* - 'The anguish of a defeat is most severely felt when we look upon weak ones who have made preparations for our victory.' Hitherto no biographer has seemed to think this note requires explanation. It is dated August 1865 - the very time at which we may now suppose Hardy had just been forced to return home defeated. The 'weak ones' look like the members of the Bockhampton household who in this August must witness what at that moment would have looked very like the collapse of the architectural career in which they had invested so much.

We seem to have discovered a second new fact about Hardy's biography to set beside the date of his final parting from Tryphena Sparks. In the 1867 when he claims to have been severely ill there is compelling evidence that he was not. When we look for an alternative year there is diverse but curiously consistent evidence that points to the real date of the illness which forced him from work in London as 1865. I have not yet exhausted the consistencies.

IX - THE MATTERHORN

July 1865 did not just see the homecoming of an obscure architect's assistant - it also witnessed a tragedy on the international stage. On 14 July 1865 the first ascent of the Matterhorn turned to disaster when a rope broke and four of the seven climbers who had conquered the peak fell to their deaths on the descent. The dead were three gentlemen climbers and their guide. *Life* dates the crisis of Hardy's severe illness to the end of July. But if, as it now appears, this was the late July of 1865 the climax of his illness must more or less have coincided with the tragedy on the Matterhorn. This is a connection Hardy makes in the very first set-piece of his very first published novel.

In *Desperate Remedies* the architect Ambrose Graye suffers a lengthy period of feeling 'lonely and depressed', of 'moody nervousness' and 'indescribable depression'. This affliction leads directly to his death when he distractedly falls from a church spire. The fall itself seems rather knowingly modeled on the disaster on the Matterhorn. The spire is described as an 'airy summit' and on it - in addition to Graye in his dark office suit - are four working-men in white, 'three masons and a mason's labourer'. This detail faithfully preserves the distinction between the three gentlemen-climbers and their guide who died in the fall on the Matterhorn. Appropriately they make their tiny movements 'with a soft, spirit-like silentness.' A sense of scale is given by the fact 'that they were indifferent to - even unconscious of - the distracted world beneath them, and all that moved upon it.'

The scene of Ambrose Graye's fall from the spire is in fact saturated with hints of the Alpine tragedy. Just as the father steps back and his foot slips, so his daughter Cytherea 'unknowingly stood, as it were, on the extreme posterior edge of a tract in her life.' Or there is Cytherea's view of the spire 'framed in by the dark margin of the window, the keen-edged shadiness of which emphasized by contrast the softness of the objects enclosed' which was surely suggested to Hardy by the report in the *Times* which described following the movements of the distant climbers through a telescope.[11]

With Ambrose Graye's death his architectural practice collapses. As a consequence we next see his son Owen traveling to Dorset by train on a July day which is 'one of the most glowing that the climax of a long series of summer heats could evolve'. This and the detailed description of hot summer weather looks like an evocation of the exceptional meteorological conditions of the historical 1865. In the illness, the Matterhorn, the failure as an architect and the departure for Dorset, Hardy seems to have sketched out what now appears to have been the sequence of salient events in the crisis of 1865. The narrative method looks like an anticipation of the sort of thing he was to do later in precisely placing the death of the first

---

[11] I assume Hardy was alerted - if not electrified - by this detail because he had witnessed the hanging of James Seale *through a telescope* - the contrast of the hanged man's white clothing and the dark clothes of the officials on that occasion suggests that this recollection was Hardy's cue for the exact conception of Ambrose Graye's fall from the spire and shows how consciously he has adapted the memory to characterise the three gentlemen climbers and their guide who died on the Matterhorn.

Avice in *The Well-Beloved* in the context of a series of events from his own life.

Hardy returns to the story of 1865 in *An Indiscretion*. A lengthy period of 'gloominess of mind' and 'low spirits and mental uneasiness' leads to the death of old Farmer Broadford. The means of death is a fall - the farmer falls from a rick when a ladder breaks under him. The broken ladder stands in for the broken rope on the Matterhorn, for Farmer Broadford's fall, dated as it is just prior to August 1865 in the calendar of the story, exactly coincides with the date of the Alpine tragedy. His illness has just the same symptoms as that of Ambrose Graye.

These are also the symptoms which lead up to the death of Old South in *The Woodlanders*. The old man's progressive debility is due to his obsession. The sight of the tall elm tree rocking before his window creates 'the terrifying illusion' in the woodman's mind that the tree intends to claim his life - 'This fear it apparently was, rather than any organic disease, which was eating away the health of John South.' But once more there seems to be an evocation of the Matterhorn disaster. There is the Alpine scale - Winterborne 'climbing higher into the sky, and cutting himself off more and more from all intercourse with the sublunary world...' until 'he could only just be discerned as a dark grey spot on the light grey zenith' - or the deft aside, when the tree falls, that anybody 'could now set foot on marks formerly made in the upper forks by the shoes of adventurous climbers only.'[12]

It is not credible that Hardy should connect hints of the Matterhorn disaster with the same protracted depressive illness three times over by pure chance. The repeated connection confirms the dating of Hardy's severe illness to 1865 - the date explicitly offered by *An Indiscretion*. No doubt the Matterhorn supplied Hardy with other cues. The scene where Knight and Elfride cling to the brow of the cliff was surely prompted by it - the scene is set in the summer of 1865 after all. Even the bucket Clym retrieves from Captain Vye's well - in the same summer 1865 of the calendar - has a hint of the Alpine tragedy. Precisely seven men are straining on a rope like the seven men roped together on the Matterhorn. Clym is a young man of twenty-five in the summer 1865 of *The Return of the Native* and, as we have seen, Hardy lets the cat out of the bag in admitting that he has been severely ill. The Matterhorn does not

---

[12] It looks pretty certain that some narrative phase of *The Poor Man* anticipated these 'Matterhorn' scenes of the later novels. They have a complex of tell-tale details in common. There are the parallel vignettes of examining the unhelpful papers in the *escritoires* of Ambrose Graye and Farmer Broadford. There are the identical reactions of Cytherea and South to the moment of crisis - rising up speechless and falling back. There is the paragraph, where two of the three narratives come closest to identity, which pictures Mayne and Winterborne sitting alone at home contemplating their older relation's death - each with its clock, its man-servant, its moonlight and its coffin in a room upstairs. There is also the closeness of effect of the phrases 'the distracted world beneath' and 'the sublunary world' which open out an Alpine scale in both *Desperate Remedies* and *Woodlanders*. At the onset of Farmer Broadford's depression we read 'The transplanting of old people is like the transplanting of old trees: a twelvemonth usually sees them wither and die away.' This may well have been the germ of Hardy's treatment of Old South's neurosis in *Woodlanders* and thus a further hint as to the common origin of these narratives.

merely confirm 1865 as the date at which Hardy's illness forced him to return home, it helps us to understand what sort of an illness he had.

X - A DIAGNOSIS

With Ambrose Graye, Farmer Broadford and Old South there is an extraordinary consistency of symptoms. The 'moody nervousness' or 'indescribable depression' or 'uneasiness of mind' is spread over a lengthy period of time but leads to a breaking point which coincides with the Matterhorn disaster. It is fear 'rather than any organic disease' which eats away at the health of Old South and the psychic nature of his illness is brilliantly caught in making the tree which terrifies him exactly his own age and therefore an *alter ego* so that his disease is a terror of himself. This is the inner picture. Physically there is the pallor and the weakness - the shocking pallor and loss of strength Hardy describes in *Life*. These are symptoms already conjoined in the 1866 poem 'Her Dilemma' whose hero is 'so wan and worn that he could scarcely stand' and in the account of Owen Graye's illness set in a calendar of summer 1865. The twenty-five year old Somerset brings a paleness of face with him from the city and so does the twenty-five year old Clym. The pallor is the outward manifestation of the inner anxiety - it is the pallor of depressive anxiety.

The 'moody nervousness' on which our three fictional accounts agree gives a clue to the looming significance of the Matterhorn. The accident to the mountaineers is a moment of terror, a moment to which it seems the depressed Hardy of the summer of 1865 was already sensitively attuned. The hint of such an attunement is to be found in the prose sketch 'How I Built Myself a House' which Hardy had written by the end of 1864. The young architect's assistant who is narrator of the sketch is terrified at 'the sight of cliffs, roofs, scaffolding, and elevated places in general, which have no sides to keep people from slipping off.' He experiences this terror to the full when he has to climb up a scaffolding to inspect the chimneys of his new house. The scene is the climax of the tale and despite its comic touch the young architect's terror has a realism that suggests a predisposition in the young Hardy to find the Matterhorn disaster an inordinately shocking event. It enables us to see what Hardy meant by setting the figure of Ambrose Graye in a dark office suit such as he wore himself as an architect's assistant beside the white, spirit-like figures of the men who had died on the Matterhorn. In some sense Hardy, the assistant church architect, sees himself in this persona who embodies his illness of 1865 reeling and doubling off the airy summit of the church spire.

The consistency of the symptoms of Ambrose Graye, Farmer Broadford and Old South and the connection of all three with the disaster on the Matterhorn strongly suggest that Hardy's illness of the summer of 1865 was a state of uncontrolled anxiety. It is in this context that news of the Alpine disaster may merely have offered the *coup de grace* to Blomfield's young assistant. If the illness and death of Farmer Broadford, set just before August 1865 in the calendar of *An Indiscretion*, is taken as a commentary on Hardy's own illness of that year, the thoughtful reflections of the farmer's grandson point to such an interpretation. Egbert Mayne considers that it was his grandfather's fall from the broken ladder - that minimal indication of the tragedy on the Matterhorn - that 'hastened by a few months a dissolution which would soon have taken place under any circumstances'. This is the sort of timescale *Life* has in mind, where Hardy's debility increased 'month by month'. The news from the Alps raises anxiety to terror, but it is the anxiety which would have brought a climax to the illness 'under any circumstances'.

We do not have far to look for the effective causes of Hardy's anxiety. In *Life* he describes himself as 'an isolated student cast on the billows of London with no protection but his brains'. In a projected speech for *The Society of Dorset Men in London* he speaks of the 'feeling of gloomy isolation' of his early London years. He seems to see gloom and isolation as natural concomitants. His sporadic letters to his sister Mary show a falling graph from news of friends in his early months in London to an absence of any mention of them. Ambrose Graye is 'lonely and depressed', a man with no friends, who comes to be 'not so tenderly regarded' by the acquaintances that he does have. In 'The Two Men' of 1866, a poem which seems to have so much to tell us of Hardy's mental state in the summer of 1865, the young man 'living long so closely penned....had not kept a single friend.'

In those narrative moments through which the outline of the Matterhorn looms the theme of isolation is inescapable. It is spelled out in great detail in the portrait of Ambrose Graye. In *Woodlanders* the theme is given to Fitzpiers in that narrative span which directly leads up to the fall of Old South's tree. Fitzpiers lives in 'insulated solitude' and his midnight 'lucubrations' look very much like a transposition of Hardy's recollection of shutting himself up in his lodgings 'every evening from six to twelve reading incessantly'. There is a glimpse into Hardy's workshop here. The autobiographical moment seems to be parceled out among several personae. Hardy makes this phase of the narrative into a pretty complete account of the crisis of July 1865 by giving Old South his illness, Fitzpiers the isolation that led to the illness and Winterborne the loss of livelihood that resulted from it. *Desperate Remedies* had already inaugurated such a scheme. Here the illness of 1865 is given to the older Ambrose Graye and the loss of livelihood that results from it to his son Owen who takes on himself an additional presentation of Hardy's severe illness - now at its correct date in the calendar of the novel. In *An Indiscretion* the crisis of 1865 is parceled out between the old farmer and his grandson.

If we draw together the implications of the climactic scene of 'How I Built Myself a House' and the 1866 sonnet 'In Vision I Roamed' it is possible to see how directly loneliness relates to anxiety. At the moment of maximum dread the young husband inspecting his chimneys in the prose sketch sees his wife 'picking daisies a little distance off, apparently in a state of complete indifference as to whether I was on the scaffold, at the foot of it, or in St. George's Hospital.' This is the comic version. In 'In Vision I

Roamed' the inert diction of 'ghast heights' and 'monstrous dome' obscures the fact that this is our earliest glimpse of those 'stellar glides' which reach a fearful apotheosis in *Two on a Tower*. It is at this moment of maximum disjunction that 'the sick grief that you were far away/Grew pleasant thankfulness that you were near.' In the prose sketch the distance between the scaffolding and the ground and the emotional distance of the woman are two expressions of the same thing. The same equivalence is implied by the sonnet 'In Vision I Roamed', where the terror of physical distance is compensated for by the woman's emotional nearness. The climax of Hardy's illness in London in 1865 expresses his distance from any emotional attachment. His defeat - the fact that he had to return home - is an admission of his inability to continue living without intimacy. His 'lateness of development in virility' is a repression which is unlocked by illness. The illness leaves him incapable of rejecting his cure. And here, on cue, the maiden of the 'She, to Him' sonnets appears.

XI - MIXED CHRISTMAS PARTIES

Was the maiden of the 'She, to Him' sonnets Hardy's young cousin Tryphena Sparks? In late July 1865 when Hardy returned home to Bockhampton she was a girl of fourteen and a half. It is this youthfulness at this precise date which turns out to be one of the prime keys to the identity which lurks behind the façade of a number of the narratives Hardy has dated to 1865.

Such youthfulness may be quite straightforwardly represented. When the calendar has reached the summer of 1865 in *A Pair of Blue Eyes* Elfride attempts her daredevil walk on the parapet of the church tower. Knight reflects on it in his pocket book - 'Girl gets into her teens, and her self-consciousness is born.....Generally begins career by actions that are popularly termed showing off.' Knight cites the escapade on the tower as such an action. So Elfride is just beginning her career of feminine self-consciousness. Should we accept the logic of Knight's pocket-book entry that she has just got into her teens? Evidently, for this is precisely her own conclusion - 'You alluded to me in that entry as if I were such a child, too. Everybody does that. I cannot understand it. I am quite a woman, you know.' On the surface of the narrative Elfride is a young lady of nineteen, but this little episode seems to hint that she is a much younger girl. This is surely why Hardy has made Knight apply the obscure word *infantine* to Elfride - an allusion to Shelley's description of the child/woman Cythna in *The Revolt of Islam* as 'A child most infantine.' In Shelley's extraordinary conception she is the hero Laon's twelve year old mistress. Later, in *Woodlanders*, a stanza describing Cythna - 'She moved upon this earth a shape of brightness' - is to be applied to Grace Melbury. Later still, in *Jude*, the comparison of Jude and Sue's relationship with that of Laon and Cythna is once again emphatic. The point to be stressed is that the calendar of *A Pair of Blue Eyes* has now reached the summer of 1865. It is at this juncture that Elfride seems only just to have got into her teens. In the summer of

1865 Tryphena Sparks was a girl of scarcely fourteen and a half.

The same 1865 calendar underlies the first part of *An Indiscretion* when we read of Geraldine 'She looked not much more than a child now,' or when she speaks 'in the sanguine tones of a child' or, even more explicitly, when she refers back to that romance which the narrative dates to 1865 in words which exactly match those of Elfride - 'I was such a child at that time, you know.' Once more it is at a date of summer 1865 that Geraldine appears as 'such a child'.

More recondite hints of such youthfulness may underlie other fictions which have a calendar of 1865. There is *The Return of the Native* which dates Clym and Eustacia's romance to the summer of 1865. At the Boxing Day dance at Bloom's End of the preceding Christmastime Eustacia goes to Mrs. Yeobright's house as one of the mummers. As the Turkish Knight she is disguised as a boy who speaks with a 'juvenile and fluty' voice and it is only at the climax of the scene that Clym penetrates her disguise when he asks 'Are you a woman?' It will be illuminating to put a date to this party at Bloom's End.

Hardy is careful with his calendar. The chapter that describes Mrs. Yeobright's journey across the heath opens with the words 'Thursday, the thirty-first of August...' In 1865 the thirty-first of August fell on a Thursday and the description of the exceptionally hot summer weather to which Clym's mother succumbs looks like an accurate recollection of the 'Italian summer' of 1865. At the very opening of the action in the previous year we are told that the fifth of November fell on a Saturday. It fell on a Saturday in 1864. When the narrative reaches the end of this year we are told that Mrs. Yeobright's party falls on a Monday which is two or three days after the twenty-third of December. We are told that the day is Monday three times over. This was Boxing Day, which fell on a Monday in 1864.

A diary of the 1860s survives written by Albert Brett, a schoolteacher and native of Puddletown who was returning home for the holidays. He records meeting Hardy at the Sparks' house in Puddletown on the evening of Boxing Day 1864. Precisely this Boxing Day 1864 in the calendar of *The Return of the Native* is the evening of the dance at Bloom's End at which the mummers perform and at which Clym meets Eustacia. The episode has distinct connections with the Sparks' house in Puddletown. In his reminiscences Nathaniel Sparks Jnr. stated that that house had a fuel-house at the back where mummers' plays were rehearsed. In the novel there is a fuel-house attached to the heroine's home where the mummers rehearse - among them a Jim Starks who is a pretty thin disguise for Tryphena's brother James Sparks. The fact that the Sparks' house appears to be evoked on the very Boxing Day 1864 on which Hardy had visited it in real life is too startling for coincidence.

Does this Boxing Day 1864 appear elsewhere in the fictions? It looks pretty certain that it is also the one recalled in *Under the Greenwood Tree* where we see the light-footed Fancy Day dancing at the tranter's party. These scenes at the tranter's were lifted from *The Poor*

Man - Macmillan's reader, John Morley, referred to 'the opening pictures of the Christmas Eve in the tranter's house' - and the calendar of the lost novel appears to have begun at Christmas 1864, as does that of its stepchild *An Indiscretion*. Fancy Day is given Tryphena's profession of teaching - even her unusual route into the profession by a Queen's Scholarship - and with her plentiful bunches of dark brown hair and brows like 'two slurs in music' we may agree with Gittings that 'her brunette beauty certainly corresponds in general with photographs of Tryphena.' There is also the curiously laboured circumstance of old William's absolute refusal to let the dance at which Fancy appears with her gliding motion begin before the midnight of Christmas Day - so that it begins on Boxing Day!

There is no escaping these Christmas parties. The central romance of *Desperate Remedies* is explicitly set in the summer of 1865, but at her very first appearance some very precise ages are given for the young heroine Cytherea.

> At mixed Christmas parties, when she numbered but twelve or thirteen years, and was heartily despised on that account by lads who deemed themselves men, her apt lightness in the dance covered this incompleteness in her womanhood, and compelled the self-same youths in spite of resolutions to seize upon her childish figure as a partner they could not afford to contemn.

In December 1863 Hardy wrote to his sister Mary that he expects to be home just after Christmas and looks forward to a 'bit of a lark'. At the next Christmas, that of 1864, he visited Puddletown as Albert Brett's diary informs us. At the end of October 1865, however, he writes to Mary proposing to come to her school at Denchworth over Christmas and the note 'Denth. Xmas '65' in his copy of *The Golden Treasury* confirms that he carried out the plan. Hardy was in Dorset at the Christmas of 1863 and 1864 but not in that of 1865. At Christmas 1863 and Christmas - or Boxing Day - 1864 Tryphena was respectively twelve and thirteen years old - the precise ages at which Cytherea appears at mixed Christmas parties. This finding dovetails in an extraordinary fashion with the fact that Hardy specially inscribed the dance at Bloom's End where Clym and Eustacia meet with the date of the Boxing Day 1864 on which he had visited Tryphena's home.

In all three fictional evocations of the Boxing Day visit of 1864 there is a particular idiosyncrasy which strongly suggests that Eustacia, Fancy and Cytherea were all drawn from the same original. When Cytherea is introduced her most striking characteristic is 'the gracefulness of her movement'.

> Indeed, motion was her speciality.....The carriage of her head – motion within motion - a glide upon a glide - was as delicate as that of a magnetic needle. And this flexibility or elasticity had never been taught her by rule....In childhood, a stone or stalk in the way, which had been the inevitable occasion of a fall to her playmates, had usually left her safe and upright on her feet after the narrowest escape by oscillations and whirls for the preservation of her balance.

At the tranter's Christmas party the dancing Fancy Day shares the same highly specific trait with Cytherea - 'Flexibility was her first characteristic, by which she appeared to enjoy the most easeful rest when she was in gliding motion.' It is a trait which is not forgotten with Eustacia. She too is 'Desperately fond of dancing' and it can scarcely be an accident that it is as she leaves the dance where she meets Wildeve that we read - 'the irregularities of the path were not visible, and Wildeve occasionally stumbled; whilst Eustacia found it necessary to perform some graceful feats of balancing whenever a small tuft of heath or root of furze protruded itself through the grass of the narrow track and entangled her feet.' Just so Cytherea - a stone or a stalk in the way had been her opportunity to escape 'by oscillations and whirls for the preservation of her balance.'

Can it be an accident that these close parallels occur in the context of Cytherea dancing and Eustacia just leaving a dance? Is there a glimpse of a prior text here - one that would also explain the way the words 'flexibility', 'motion' and 'glide' or 'gliding' are grouped so closely together in the accounts of both Cytherea and Fancy's *flexibility*? If this is the text of *The Poor Man* it does not follow that, for instance, the Christmas dance at the tranter's is simply lifted from the suppressed novel. In that case it would be difficult to explain what the Lady - Miss Allancourt - was doing dancing in the tranter's humble cottage. Similarly the Boxing Day party of *The Return of the Native* also has the liberty of a fictional invention. Even if Hardy is relying on recollection there is a certain plasticity in his use of it - a possibility we may glimpse in Nathaniel Sparks Jnr's tradition that Hardy had made unwanted approaches to Rebecca Sparks at a rehearsal of the mummers in Puddletown and that her mother Maria had shown Hardy the door. This incident may have enriched - or contaminated - the scene where Clym and Eustacia first meet face to face, but the surface freedom of the fiction only throws the subcutaneous constancies of calendar or repeated characterisation into sharper relief. With Mrs. Yeobright's party it is the precision of the dating to Boxing day 1864 which like a boulder breaks surface above the fictional flow.

As a repeated characteristic of all three of the heroines who project a version of the Boxing Day visit to Puddletown in 1864 it seems virtually certain that the idiosyncrasy of gliding motion was Tryphena's. It is a conclusion that seems to be confirmed by 'In a Eweleaze Near Weatherbury' where it is Tryphena who broaches the topic at the very opening of the poem -

> The years have gathered grayly
> Since I danced upon this leaze...

- a statement which alerts us to the 'gliding motion' of the dance measure which sustains the whole poem.

Just how important this quirk of gliding motion was to Hardy may be judged from the arcane device by which he generated the name of his heroine in *Desperate Remedies*. In the scene where Springrove and Cytherea take a boat on Weymouth Bay Hardy adapts a line from Gray's *Progress of Poesy* - 'The bloom of young Desire, and purple light of Love.' This becomes 'The bloom and the purple light were strong on the lineaments of both.' Hardy knows this is a quotation for after the first edition of *Desperate Remedies* he re-punctuates it - 'The 'bloom' and the 'purple light'.....' The quotation is taken from the strophe of the poem which celebrates the 'Power of harmony to produce all the graces of motion in the body' and in which the bloom and purple light belong to the goddess Cytherea. So it is for her graces of motion that the heroine is named Cytherea and given the surname Graye for Gray the poet.

The Boxing Day visit was evidently a cardinal date in Hardy's biography. On each of its fictional epiphanies it seems that it is Tryphena who makes the scene memorable. Tryphena was thirteen at the Christmas of 1864. This seems the point of recalling Cytherea as a thirteen year old at a mixed Christmas party and as a natural sequel the central romance of Cytherea's story is set in 1865. Clym and Eustacia meet at a party specifically dated to the Boxing Day 1864 on which Hardy visited the Sparks at Puddletown and Eustacia's romance with Clym is also to be set in the summer of 1865. We may suspect that the Christmas opening of *Under the Greenwood Tree* once more refers to the Christmas of 1864 since it appears to have borrowed these scenes from the suppressed *The Poor Man* which itself seems once more to have centered on a calendar of 1865. Fancy Day in her looks and her career as teacher seems clearly enough to have been inspired by Tryphena. This Christmas of 1864 is a prelude to the 1865 to which the calendars of the novels obsessively return and strongly suggests that the heroines of 1865 are a young Tryphena Sparks about to step out from the wings.

XII - SO THE PARSON SAID

Later novels only confirm the connection between a special flexibility and Tryphena. Hardy calls the young Cytherea's gracefulness of movement *flexibility* and *elasticity*. Fancy Day's 'first characteristic' is also *flexibility*. The word appears as a leitmotif in the later novels. Grace Melbury is instantly introduced as 'a flexible young creature'. Tess in the cornfield is called 'the most flexuous and finely-drawn of them all' and there is also the temporary inclusion in MS 2 of *Tess* of the words 'by looking down she avoided catching the observers' eyes, but her elasticity she could not hide'. At first sight these adjectives *flexible* and *flexuous* look like very slender evidence for a positive identification. But they do not seem to be accidental. The whole complex of meaning surrounding the naming of Cytherea is still evident in *Woodlanders*. In the manuscript a reworking of the brief allusion to Grace Melbury's marriage shows with what crystal consciousness Hardy was aware of the real meaning of his heroine's flexuousness. Grace is 'flushed by the purple light and bloom of her own passion'. The manuscript shows that Hardy first wrote 'purple light of love' in a verbatim quotation from Gray's *Progress of Poesy* from that particular strophe glossed as the 'Power of harmony to produce all the graces of motion in the body' which supplied the name of the dancing Cytherea Graye.

We are told that Grace Melbury's family name occurs in documents 'about the time of the civil wars'. In the first chapter of *Life* Hardy directly cites Hutchins' *History* to pinpoint precisely the same details about the civil war and their connection with his mother's family. Indeed, his own copy of the *History* shows pencilled underlinings of these facts about his mother's ancestry in Melbury Osmund, the village which provides Grace with her surname. Grace Melbury is also 'glorified and refined' by her schooling. Apart from Hardy's own sisters a girl of his mother's family who is good at school can - if we are thinking in terms of reality - only be Tryphena Sparks.

Once Hardy has hit on a means of identifying his heroine he cannot help elaborating it. The source for these details about Grace's family is indicated in the little aside - 'at least so the parson said'. At the very beginning of his next novel, *Tess*, Hardy refers to Hutchins' *History* by way of Parson Tringham - a transparent substitute for the Rev. Bingham, reviser of Hardy's own edition of Hutchins and so an explanation for the parson of *Woodlanders*. Tess is now provided with a Norman ancestry. Hardy's copy of the *History* also shows pencilled underlinings of the supposed Norman connections of his mother's family from Melbury Osmund. Again Tess is good at school - she is expected to go for a Pupil Teacher. But we scarcely need this additional confirmation that Hardy connected Tess with his cousin Tryphena. She is already identified with the dead Tryphena through that quotation from the journal note of 15 March 1890 of the crush at Lady Jeune's which he inserted into the jewels episode.

These cues to external reality do not tell us how to read the texts in which they occur, but they do give us an inkling as to what were the dominant images in Hardy's mind as he wrote. I began by showing that *The Well-Beloved* was saturated with the image of Tryphena. In its revised form this was Hardy's last novel. The allusion to the Boxing Day party of 1864 and the heroine's special flexibility make it look as if Tryphena also played a seminal rôle in his first published novel, *Desperate Remedies*. The concealed web of allusions I am tracing out begins to suggest that she is a constant presence behind the façade of the Wessex Novels - a finding which, it seems, is underpinned by the calendar for 1865 on which Hardy structures the novels over and over again.

XIII - BOCKHAMPTON AND THE HARDY MONUMENT

My interpretation of the calendar of *The Well-Beloved* as a late revival of the arcane system of *An Indiscretion* now seems plain sailing. The story opens in the summer of 1865 and its heroine - the first Avice - is elaborately identified with Tryphena. There is now an explanation for the anomaly that in *Life* Hardy draws attention to the illness which drove him from London, but at the same time conceals its real significance. His misdating severs the link between the illness and the year 1865. It has the effect of making 1865 what the poem 'At Rushy Pond' calls 'a secret year'. The careful camouflage with which Hardy has inserted his 1865 calendars into the novels shows that he always had wanted to make 1865 a secret year - even while, in some compulsive way, he cannot help making constant reference to it. His motive for the obfuscation may have been the fact that Tryphena was a girl of only fourteen in the summer of 1865 or perhaps a consciousness of the pathetic imbalance between a mishap of his youth and the burgeoning superstructure of the Wessex Novels. Hardy wants to conceal the story, but he cannot resist leaving us clues - such as his announcement of the identity which lies behind 'Thoughts of Phena', the assertion that the story of *Jude* has something to do with the death of a woman in 1890, or the little chronology which illustrates his 'lateness of development in virility', a trait which he explicitly calls 'a clue to much of his character and action throughout his life.'

This doubleness - the wish to conceal and the wish to show - is at work from the very beginning of Hardy's authorship. The poems of 1865-7 embody an autobiography which they also conceal. Sometimes Hardy feels he has gone too far. The greater part of the 'She, to Him' cycle had in the end to be suppressed. Or, as with the case of 'The Unplanted Primrose' which the manuscript dates 1865-67, he toyed with publication but could not finally make up his mind to it.

It is difficult in this latter case - or perhaps in any other case - to sort the showing from the concealment. The fable of 'The Unplanted Primrose' - that the girl had brought her lover a primrose he had casually failed to plant - may be more image than a report of actuality. But it is certainly an image which adumbrates a reality - the 1865-7 date of the poem and its contrast between a previous time of love 'a year before' with the lover's present neglect exactly meshes with the reproachful burden of the rest of the 'She, to Him' sonnets of 1866. The girl who spoke those sonnets calls herself Maiden. In the manuscript of 'The Unplanted Primrose' we see an elderly Hardy substituting the lamest of fillers for the word 'maiden' in a continuing effort of concealment. If the negligent lover is Hardy we know that he had not really left for 'a southern country unassayed'. In the story 'Destiny and a Blue Cloak' and in *Desperate Remedies* the departure for a 'southern country' has every appearance of being a gloss on Hardy's return to London and Blomfield's office in the autumn of 1865. But now that it seems that it is the young Tryphena who has suffered the neglect implied by her lover's failure to plant the primrose other details take on the sharp outlines of a reality outside the poem. Its maiden lives 'but a little mile' from her lover's old home which, with its 'border of early stocks,/Of pansies, pinks, and hollyhocks', is surely a vignette of the garden at Bockhampton. She appears to enter the garden unannounced, a freedom Tryphena seems to have felt towards the Bockhampton household - at least, I suppose it is her Aunt Hardy and Uncle she is referring to when she says in a letter of 1869 that she is to 'go to Bockhampton about some work, & I shall sleep there if I'm in the same mind as now.'

The 'She, to Him' sonnets are also given a touch of documentary relevance by the illustration Hardy made for them when he published them in *Wessex Poems* in 1898. The illustration shows the characteristic abacus of the monument to Admiral Hardy on Blackdown with the flint-scattered paths that wind up the hill. Millgate has another candidate for the girl of the 'She, to Him' sonnets - Eliza Nicholls - and says that the illustration is of Clavel Tower, close by Eliza's original home in Kimmeridge. But Clavel Tower, with no flint-scattered paths leading up to it, has a prominent peristyle and no abacus, while the tower of the illustration - like the Hardy Monument on Blackdown - has a distinct abacus but no peristyle.[13] Hardy the sometime architect and connoisseur of all things local would have been clear about such details - and anyway he had only to rely on his daily pilgrimage to the garden gate at Max Gate with its view of Blackdown to refresh his memory. But there is other evidence that Purdy's suggestion of Blackdown as the scene of the illustration was correct all along.

When the calendar of *An Indiscretion* reaches August 1865 a scene is pointedly set at the Hardy Monument. The location is deftly fixed by the hero and heroine's discussion of the exact mileage of the road that leads to a town visible in the distance whose name is made up of two elements of the nearest suburbs of Weymouth - the seaside town that lies in clear view of the Hardy Monument and exactly at the mileage indicated in the dialogue. Hardy's introduction of the scene at the particular 1865 date given to it in the calendar of *An Indiscretion* dovetails decisively with the illustration to

---

[13]See my article in *Thomas Hardy Society Review*, 1983, p. 271.

the 'She, to Him' sonnets which have every appearance of reflecting an affair which dated from the time of Hardy's illness in that same summer of 1865.

The Ridgeway of which Blackdown and the Hardy Monument are the western culmination also seems to be the scene of 'The Musing Maiden' - a poem written in October 1866 - in which the maiden's mind travels with the coasters she can see to what appears to be the Thames opposite the windows of Hardy's office at Adelphi Terrace.[14] In 1865 the riverside there was a forest of scaffolding, lifting gear and wharves where the coasters from Portland landed their stone. With just the same imaginative association Avice inspires Pierston to frequent the quays on the south bank of the Thames in *The Well-Beloved* because the coasters which discharge their cargoes of stone there carry his mind back to his beloved in Portland. The connection must have seemed an obvious one for the young Hardy who only had to look out of the office - 'We can see from our windows right across the Thames,' as he writes to his sister Mary - to watch the construction of the Thames Embankment in Portland stone. These details fix the scene of 'The Musing Maiden' as the Ridgeway overlooking Portland.

I have no evidence that Tryphena was associated with Blackdown and the Hardy Monument in 1865. But ten years later in 1875 she writes a letter describing her stay with Robert Spiller and his wife - 'Dear Mrs

---

[14] These coasters are visible in the sketch of Portland viewed from the Ridgeway which Hardy made from memory on the fly-leaf of his copy of Mariette's *Half-Hours of French Translation* - a textbook he was using in the winter of 1865-6.

and Mr Spiller they seemed so glad to see me - and drove me all about the place...' Indeed she makes two visits to them during her holiday. The account of her visits with their haymaking and picnics on the beach strongly suggests what Gittings calls 'a close and longstanding friendship'. The Spillers lived at Waddon on the slope of Blackdown just below the Hardy Monument. The letter is not proof that the friendship extended all the way back to 1865. But the fact that Tryphena seems to have been associated with this remote spot well before 1875 is highly suggestive. The fact that Hardy has sedulously introduced the Hardy Monument into the calendar of *An Indiscretion* at the August of 1865 only underlines the probability that her connection with the spot reaches right back to this early date.[15]

XIV - COVERT SCENES OF INTERCOURSE

The *Well-Beloved* makes it clear that it was Tryphena's death which put an end to Hardy's 'young manhood'. If some other woman had made him a young man in 1865 it is not obvious why it should have

---

[15] If Deacon and Coleman are right in connecting the poem 'My Cicely' with Tryphena the presence of the 'Nine-Pillared Cromlech' should be noted - this should be the Hell Stone (again on the southern flank of Blackdown) since it is described in Hutchins' *History* as 'a cromlech - the only one in the County'. Robert Spiller came from Stockland, now in East Devon, a parish which contained numerous households of Sparks. One of them - a John Sparks, chair-maker - was brother-in-law to a Robert Spiller of Trimshayes. If he is the uncle of our Robert Spiller this may be an explanation of how Tryphena came to be staying with the Spillers at Waddon.

been precisely Tryphena's death which released Hardy from this curious state when he was 'nearly fifty'. It would make a great deal more sense - even a tragic sense - if it was Tryphena who had inaugurated his young manhood in the first place. In the summer of 1865 she was a girl of fourteen and a half. Since Hardy speaks of becoming a young man in the context of his 'development in virility' it is at least a speculation that he had intercourse with his young cousin when he returned to Bockhampton in that summer. It would be as well to see if the fictions respond to such a guess.

A scene of intercourse is pictured in the short story 'Destiny and a Blue Cloak'. I am almost tempted to say *recorded*, for there is a documentary substratum to this story which Hardy has scarcely bothered to conceal at all. The heroine, Agatha, is a young girl of a household which is faithfully modeled on that of Tryphena's family in Puddletown. The Sparks lived in Mill Street, the house 'with the sparkling river in front', as Mary Hardy called it. In the short story the house is a Mill which 'stood beside the village high-road, from which it was separated by the stream'. Tryphena's brothers were called James and Nathaniel - the family of the story has brothers John and Nathaniel. Part of the fictional family are about to emigrate to Queensland. Such a plan must have been mooted in the Sparks family at the time Hardy wrote the story - eighteen months after its appearance Tryphena's sister Martha was to emigrate to Queensland.

The story contains a scene in which the young Agatha has intercourse beside the millstream. The act is described with a symbolism that is blatant rather than refined. Hardy seems to have in mind the country proverb he uses elsewhere - when a girl has intercourse she is said to 'tear her smock'. The elderly Farmer Lovill who is her suitor surprises the 'pretty maid' Agatha so that she lets go of the chemise she is washing and exclaims 'it will get into the wheel, and be torn to pieces!' The farmer offers to retrieve it with his stick with which he begins 'hooking and crooking with all his might'. The reader need only turn to the next page to have the sexual significance of the stick made plain to him in actions of the most extraordinary grossness. When the farmer retrieves the chemise the girl looks red, but he assures her there is no shame in owning 'such a necessary and innocent article of clothing'. He then retires 'lifting his fingers privately, to express amazement on a small scale, and murmuring, 'What a nice young thing! Well, to be sure. Yes, a nice child - young woman rather; indeed, a marriageable woman, come to that; of course she is.' This motif of the child/woman makes it clear that of all the daughters of the Sparks household in Puddletown which Hardy has so elaborately evoked in the tale, it is Tryphena who is represented by young Agatha. The nearest sister to Tryphena in age, Martha, was six years Hardy's senior and already in her thirties by the summer of 1865.[16]

Hardy has scarcely gone out of his way to conceal the inner meanings of 'Destiny and a Blue Cloak'. He has constructed a scene of intercourse with a child/woman who is a member of a household

---

[16] But it is tempting to think the jealous Frances of the story impersonates Martha Sparks whom, according to family tradition, Hardy had at first wanted to marry.

identified with that of the Sparks at Puddletown by the most circumstantial details. He would never republish the story in England and made it unviable by immediately recycling the *coup de théâtre* with which the story ends as the denouement of *The Hand of Ethelberta*.[17] But this narrative shock - where the heroine's rescuer is suddenly unmasked as her elderly suitor - is merely a peak of intensity in Hardy's treatment of the May and January theme of the young girl and the old lover that he will treat at greater length in *The Well-Beloved* and *Jude*. Tryphena was, after all, eleven years Hardy's junior. But what is extraordinary is that he chose to despatch this whole 'construction' of 'Destiny and a Blue Cloak' to America the week before his marriage to Emma Gifford. Given this date and its inner meanings the story might well be taken for an anguished cry flung at the cosmos - at least America was as far as Hardy could project it and far enough away to feel his secret was safe.

The timing of the publication - and presumably writing - of the story gives a special weight to its 'documentary' substratum. But the story which is told already has a context which seems to embed it in the records of 1865. Its summer romance and the young hero's departure for 'a southern country' is already a motif of the 1865-7 poem 'The Unplanted Primrose'

---

[17] The naming of Ethelberta's brothers and other details carry over the identification of the Sparks' household from the short story. So it is no surprise to read of Ethelberta 'The arch of the brows - like a slur in music' and set this beside the portrait of Fancy Day with her eyes 'arched by brows of so keen, slender, and soft a curve, that they resembled nothing so much as two slurs in music' - a portrait which Gittings concedes 'corresponds in general with photographs of Tryphena.'

and it is a motif which had been taken up by *A Pair of Blue Eyes* which Hardy had published in 1873 just a year before the writing of 'Destiny and a Blue Cloak'.

This is not all the novel and the story have in common. The very casually disguised meaning of the scene beside the millstream can now be traced back into the cliff scene of the summer of 1865 in the calendar of *A Pair of Blue Eyes*. The proverb 'to tear her smock' already informs this scene where Knight clings desperately to the cliff edge which, given the date of the concealed calendar, is surely a further reminiscence of the Matterhorn. Knight feels a 'gratified amazement' when he discovers that Elfride has torn up her petticoat to make the rope that saves him and Elfride's face is seen 'doubling its red, with an expression between gladness and shame.' This is the same Elfride who is just such a child/woman as Agatha, the Elfride who, when the novel's calendar has reached the summer of 1865, complains that Knight has described her 'as if I were such a child......I cannot understand it. I am quite a woman, you know.'

The key that 'Destiny and a Blue Cloak' offers to the inner meaning of the cliff scene gives a particular significance to Elfride's reaction at Knight's embrace - 'Every nerve of her will was now in entire subjection to her feeling - volition as a guiding power had forsaken her.' The same note is struck in the 1865 of the calendar of *Desperate Remedies* when Cytherea, pursued by Manston, stands in the 'wet old garden' choked with mandrakes - 'She felt as one in a boat without oars, drifting with closed eyes down a river - she knew not whither.' We may take these expressions of Elfride and

Cytherea's 'feeling' as mid-Victorian code for the sexual act - or at least as Hardy's code for it. It was two decades before he could be as explicit as he is in 'On the western Circuit' or *Tess*, but it is these later fictions which confirm the real significance of Cytherea's sensation of 'drifting with closed eyes down a river'.

They confirm it by the very conscious deployment of the brilliant image of the sunset gnats. I have already touched on these gnats as a reliable date-marker for 1865. They make their first published appearance in the scene where Cytherea stands in the 'wet old garden', pressed by Manston to accept him as a husband, with her mandrakes and her sensation of 'drifting with closed eyes down a river - she knew not whither.' This is the cue for the image of the gnats to appear in all its glory. It is just before sunset and 'All dark objects on the earth that lay towards the sun were overspread by a purple haze, against which a swarm of wailing gnats shone forth luminously, rising upward and floating away like sparks of fire.'

The passage is undoubtedly drawn from *The Poor Man* for as Rutland pointed out an extensive doublet of it appears in *The Return of the Native* where Clym meets Eustacia amid the ferns.

> All dark objects on the earth that lay towards the sun were overspread by a purple haze against which groups of wailing gnats shone out, rising upwards and dancing about like sparks of fire.

Once again a marriage is in question, but in the later fictions these gnats betoken a seduction. The hero of 'On the Western Circuit' wins Anna 'body and soul'.

On the eve of her seduction the young girl appears on the steam roundabout on which the riders are seen moving up and down 'like gnats against a sunset'. The image seems almost casually introduced but it is underpinned by an extraordinarily arcane device. The atmosphere of the fair in its colour and flame is likened to the eighth chasm of the *Inferno*. When we turn to Dante we find the myriad points of flame of this eighth chasm are likened in an elaborate simile to gnats at sunset. This recondite reduplication shows just how conscious and artificial Hardy's use of this symbolism is.[18]

The deployment of the gnats is equally carefully controlled in *Tess*. They put in their appearance on the eve of Tess's seduction by Alec d'Urberville. There is here a highly conscious reworking of the text of *The Poor Man*. It is 'just before sunset' and 'the atmosphere itself forms a prospect without aid from more solid objects, except the innumerable winged insects that dance in it.' This is a precise transformation of the doublet of the sunset gnats. What *Tess* words as a 'low-lit mistiness' forms an atmosphere which obscures solid objects and against which the gnats gleam distinctly - the gnats even 'dance' in this atmosphere, just as the gnats of *The Return of the Native* are 'dancing about like sparks of fire'. The special lighting is prolonged beyond sunset. A page later the dance in the barn produces 'a mist of yellow radiance' and at Tess's actual seduction the sky is held by 'a faint luminous fog'. The

---

[18] It seems safest to say *symbolism*, though the gnats and the purple haze may of course have been a direct recollection of something witnessed in the summer of 1865.

consciousness of the working becomes indisputable with Tess's final capitulation to Clare in the meads at Talbothays. Once again it is a question of marriage. The two are 'never out of the sound of some purling weir...while the beams of the sun, almost as horizontal as the mead itself, formed a pollen of radiance over the landscape.' On the verge of her capitulation to Clare we read, 'Gnats, knowing nothing of their brief glorification, wandered across the shimmer of this pathway, irradiated as if they bore fire within them.' Hardy is now certainly reworking materials of *The Poor Man* - the meads, the low sun and the shadows of Angel and Tess stretching a quarter of a mile before them are details which appeared in conjunction with the sunset gnats in *The Return of the Native* in the summer 1865 of its calendar. In the text of *Desperate Remedies* the gnats 'shone forth luminously' - in the cognate passage of *Tess* Hardy's manuscript shows that his first thought was 'Luminous gnats'. The gnats now illuminate the real meaning of the scene where Cytherea stands in the 'wet old garden' where the water gurgles down 'under the cloak of rank broad leaves - the sensuous natures of the vegetable world.'

Such a conscious reworking also informs the two uncannily similar settings of scenes amid the ferns in *Far From the Madding Crowd* and *The Return of the Native*. In the second of these - this is where the doublet of the sunset gnats makes its bold appearance - Clym and Eustacia have their rendezvous amid the ferns when they decide to marry. The episode does not immediately look like a scene of seduction until we compare it with the account of Troy's sword-play in the chapter called 'The Hollow Amid the Ferns' in *Far From the Madding Crowd*. Here there is the same early summer green of the ferns, the same position of the low sun, the same sensual brushing of garments on the ferns as Bathsheba or Eustacia attend their rendezvous. In *Far From the Madding Crowd* a reminiscence of the passage describing the sunset gnats is certainly present too. At the climax of the scene the gnats which, in one version of our original doublet, 'shone forth luminously....like sparks of fire' become the gleams of Troy's sword-blade. These flash with 'Beams of light caught from the low sun's rays', surrounding Bathsheba like 'a sky-full of meteors' - 'Behind the luminous streams of this *aurora militaris*, she could see the hue of Troy's sword arm, spread in a scarlet haze over the space covered by its motions.' Given the parallels of context in which these words appear they are too close to the luminous gnats and to the phrase 'overspread by a purple haze' for accident.

Troy's sword exercise is certainly a scene of seduction. The imagery of 'The Hollow Amid the Ferns' describes sexual intercourse in the most intimate succession of details, summarised at the start of the next chapter as a folly 'introduced as lymph on the dart of Eros'. It seems reasonable to read such a subtext into Clym and Eustacia's rendezvous amid the ferns. Eustacia is one who loves 'too hotly to love long', there is 'a certain glad and voluptuous air of triumph' in her eyes and in the immediate wake of the gnats she feels an anxious dread that 'it will get afloat that I am not a good girl.' Clym's sense of the 'oppressive horizontality' of the scene might even be taken for an expression of sexual depletion as Eustacia leaves him and the rustle of her dress dies away across the sedge.[19]

The sunset gnats explicitly mark a scene of seduction in the later fictions 'On the Western Circuit' and *Tess*. But clearly they already had such a connotation in Troy's sword exercise. By extension we can interpret Clym and Eustacia's rendezvous in the same light - and Cytherea's encounter with Manston in the wet old garden. The gnats are now a marker for a seduction. We have already seen that they are also a date-marker for 1865. So they converge upon a seduction of 1865. The heroines whom the gnats attend have only to be identified with Tryphena Sparks to make the case for the fictions recurring over and over again to a scene in which Tryphena is seduced in 1865. Cytherea is identified with Tryphena as a girl seen at mixed Christmas parties in her twelfth and thirteenth years and by her speciality of gliding motion. Tess is identified with Tryphena by covert allusions to her teaching, by her special 'flexuousness', by her ancestry reflecting Hardy's annotations in his copy of Hutchins' *History* and most explicitly by the incorporation of the journal note printed in *Life* which connects her with Tryphena's death in March 1890. Eustacia has the same special flexibility attributed to Cytherea and for Clym

---

[19] Hardy reworked these materials very closely. At Eustacia's departure she is wrapped in the sunset's 'luminous rays'. So Hardy has changed the 'shone forth luminously' of the doublet as it originally appeared in *Desperate Remedies* to a simple 'shone forth' so that he could redeploy the word *luminous* as 'luminous rays'. Clym's sense of 'oppressive horizontality' also introduces a doublet shared with the 'wet old garden' scene in *Desperate Remedies* where it is now Cytherea who feels 'a sense of bare equality with, and no superiority to, a single entity under the sky.'

she is first seen as a woman at the dance which the novel's calendar attributes to the precise Boxing Day 1864 on which Hardy visited the Sparks' house. It now seems pretty clear why Agatha, the girl seduced by the millstream in 'Destiny and a Blue Cloak' with its array of allusions to the Sparks' household, is meticulously characterised as a child/woman.

In that short story the scene of intercourse is scarcely veiled. Such an unvarnished scene forms the climax of the first phase of *The Well-Beloved*. The intercourse of Pierston and Marcia takes place under the lerret where the pair shelter from the storm. Hardy uses a wholly excessive battery of allusion to make the point that they have sex under the upturned boat. The boat forms a sort of artificial cave so that Hardy can introduce Virgil's *commixta grandine nimbus* - the rain mixed with hail which drives Dido and Aeneas into the shelter of their cave - or the seminal rain that falls 'like corn thrown in handfuls by some colossal sower' once Pierston and Marcia are under the lerret or the addition of the Miltonic quotation in the 1897 version of the novel which draws attention to the issue of sanguine humour 'such as Celestial spirits may bleed.' The point did not really need to be so elaborately made, for Marcia has already turned up at the last moment as substitute for the first Avice with whom Pierston was expecting to have intercourse - 'the custom of the Isle' - that very evening.

In any case we are already privy to the inner workings of the scene under the lerret. A single identity lurks behind the figures of both Avice and Marcia. Avice is to be heavily identified with Tryphena by the circumstances surrounding her death and at the very end of the novel Marcia as the heroine of 'The Revisitation' turns out to be one more of the masks of Tryphena. The novel's calendar sets the scene under the lerret in 1865 so that it is entirely intelligible that at this juncture Hardy should say of Marcia - 'though she was such a fine figure....she was not much more than a schoolgirl in years.'

The evidence of the fictions is conclusive. There is nothing vague or indefinite about it. Each time we are presented with a scene of covert intercourse the narrative is enriched with those private memoranda of the date and the identity of the girl which Hardy makes for himself - memoranda the reader is not expected to penetrate. Once that underlay of biographical reference is isolated it becomes clear that Hardy is repeating a simple story with massive consistency. From such certainty it may even be permissible to speculate a little. The sunset gnats and the implication of a seduction are regularly coupled with a proposal of marriage - with Manston and Cytherea, with Clym and Eustacia, with Angel and Tess. Intercourse and a proposal of marriage have become equivalents. This seems to be what the gnats imply, for they are made to appear both at the moment Alec seduces Tess and at the moment Angel at last gains Tess's assent to his proposal of marriage. But of course this is the plain significance of the 'Island Custom' in which intercourse is a pre-nuptial contract. The same concept of sexual relations was once also present in *Tess*. In an aside which did not survive the 1892 edition of the novel Tess understands of Alec that 'In a brute sense he alone was her husband.' In such a brute sense Hardy may well have felt intercourse had turned his young cousin into a *de facto* wife. The 1866 poem 'To a Bridegroom' strongly suggests that this was precisely what he did feel.

XV - MORE OF A WOMAN IN APPEARANCE THAN IN YEARS

The seemingly casual aside that Marcia though 'such a fine figure...was little more than a schoolgirl in years' is a key to what is ultimately the weightiest piece of evidence that the story of 1865 involves intercourse with a young girl. The aside about Marcia is a formula. On a number of occasions Hardy reduces important revelations to a formula - as he does with *flexibility* and *flexuousness* or the formula of his 'constitutional tendency to care for life only as an emotion and not as a scientific game' which he repeats over and over again in his autobiography.

The formula in question first appears in the 1865 calendar of *An Indiscretion* as a stray remark about its heroine Geraldine - 'from the fineness of her figure she looked more womanly than she really was.'

In *The Well-Beloved* we read that Avice the Third is 'altogether finer in figure than her mother or grandmother had ever been, which made her more of a woman in appearance than in years.' This aside was specially inserted into the rewritten 1897 version of the novel.

It is a formula that had also appeared in *Tess*. When Alec d'Urberville first sets eyes on Tess she has 'a luxuriance of aspect, a fullness of growth, which made her appear more of a woman than she really was.' When her mother dresses her up to catch the eye of Alec d'Urberville the airy frock 'imparted to her developing figure an amplitude which belied her age, and might cause her to be estimated as a woman when she was not much more than a child.' With Tess this is the key to the disaster of her young life. This being 'more of a woman in appearance than in years' is a fatal characteristic - as much a 'speciality' as the gliding motion - for it explains how a young girl gets seduced.

Once we re-read the opening of *The Well-Beloved* it looks very much as if this same characteristic is the whole basis of that misunderstanding when Pierston winces at the first Avice's impulsive kiss. The kiss was a child's, but it has taken on the significance of a woman's. Her mother says, 'Don't you know that you've grown up to be a woman since Jocelyn...was last down here?' Avice confesses, 'I - I didn't think about how I was altered,' and then, 'I quite forgot how much I had grown.' With the first Avice this seems once more to be the same 'fullness of growth' or 'fineness of figure' which leads Geraldine or Tess or the third Avice to appear 'more womanly than she really was.'

But it is only with Tess that Hardy fully unfolds the meaning of his formula. It is only with Tess that the tragic function of this disparity between age and precocious physical development is fully explored as that trick of circumstance which leads to her seduction. With Marcia no causal link is made between her 'fine figure' while still a schoolgirl and her intercourse with Pierston - though the two facts are integral parts of the same scene. Hardy's late fictions are more explicit on the subject of sex, but Geraldine - the earliest of his girls who 'looked more womanly than she really was' - evidently has the same sexual proclivities as Tess.

Weber notes of the rain that attends the schoolroom scene in *An Indiscretion* that 'we may see an echo of the famous rain that influenced the lives of Aeneas and Dido.' Hardy was also to make an extraordinary last minute revision to the start of the scene by inserting the words 'when a passionate liking for [the hero's] society was creeping over the reckless though pure girl, slowly, insidiously, and surely, like ripeness over fruit.' So Geraldine is not only like Tess in being 'more of a woman in appearance than in years' but also pre-figures the Tess who notoriously appears on the title page of her own novel as 'A Pure Woman'.[20]

The formula 'more of a woman in appearance than in years' does not stand in isolation - it is part of a more complex consistency which cannot be detached from biographical reality. It describes Geraldine in the summer of 1865 which was the summer in which Hardy reached the age of twenty-five - the age at which he claims to have become a young man. *The Well-Beloved* uses precisely the same chronological device as

---

[20] In the school scene of *An Indiscretion* Geraldine's 'soft body yielded like wool under his embrace...Egbert's feeling as he retired was that he had committed a crime.' This seems too minimal an indication that this is a covert scene of intercourse until one notices the misquotation 'harmful deed' from Shakespeare sonnet 111 as the revised epigraph to the chapter - a misquotation which throws great weight on Egbert's 'crime'. The story dates from 1878. In 1877 serious Parliamentary debate had begun about legislation which led to the modern law on the age of consent which, for practical purposes, had hitherto stood at the age of twelve.

that by which Hardy had fixed the calendar of *An Indiscretion* and here, once again, the date of its opening scenes - and therefore that of Pierston and Marcia's intercourse under the lerret - is 1865. It is at this particular date that these young heroines appear more womanly than they really are - that is, as young girls who because of their premature physical development look ripe to be seduced.

Tryphena's age correlates with this date. In 1865 she was certainly a young girl and repeatedly the young girl who is more of a woman in appearance than in years is identified with Tryphena. The first Avice - who forgets 'how much I had grown' - is elaborately identified with her by the details with which Hardy has surrounded her death. The third Avice - 'more of a woman in appearance than in years' in Hardy's special 1897 insertion - is equated with this first Avice as 'the very she....who had kissed him forty years before' and if we doubt that the cyclic procedures of the novel have brought round the 'same' identity, there are those casual details like the French course book that is lent to this third Avice. Tess - who appears 'more of a woman than she really was' - is also in some sense a surrogate for Tryphena as I have shown in Hardy's special insertion of a quotation from his journal note of 15 March 1890 into the jewels episode and in his reference to the genealogy of his mother's family, reflected in the pencilled annotations in his copy of Hutchins' *History*. Then there is Marcia of whom we read 'though she was such a fine figure...she was not much more than a schoolgirl in years'. She too is identified with Tryphena as the heroine who borrows her dramatically ruined looks from 'The Revisitation', the poem which is perhaps Hardy's earliest substantial memorial to his dead cousin. Indeed, Marcia as the girl who has sex under the lerret in a calendar of 1865 and as the woman of 'The Revisitation' unites what must now be seen as two of the cardinal dates in Hardy's experience of Tryphena - the 1865 in which he had intercourse with her and the 1890 of her death.

These interlocking consistencies leave no doubt that Tryphena Sparks was the young girl who made her cousin a 'young man' in the summer of 1865. Her youthfulness appears to be a tragic complication which goes far to explaining the hold that this misadventure of his mid twenties was to have on Hardy - a hold which makes this story a persistent inspiration of the Wessex Novels. It need hardly be said that the formula 'more of a woman in appearance than in years' is an exculpation. It was because the girl looked older than she really was that the young man had intercourse with her. That is his excuse. The photographic record of young Tryphena is not sufficiently complete to make any objective assessment, if such a thing were possible. But, of course, such judgments are subjective as we see from the Farmer hooking and crooking with Agatha beside the mill stream in 'Destiny and a Blue Cloak'. Sexual desire or performance transforms the girl before our eyes. So the Farmer retires saying, 'What a nice young thing! Well, to be sure. Yes, a nice child - young woman rather; indeed, a marriageable woman, come to that; of course she is.'

A fine figure is not the only attribute that makes a young girl seem more womanly than she really is.

When we see Cytherea Graye at a mixed Christmas party at the age of thirteen it is her 'apt lightness in the dance' which covers the 'incompleteness in her womanhood' and *compels* youths to 'seize upon her childish figure'. Is it only by accident that this wording has a sexual tinge? In this reference to Cytherea it seems quite certain that Hardy has in mind the Boxing Day party of 1864 which is pinpointed in the calendar of *The Return of the Native.* Was it now that Hardy had his first intimation of a sexual attraction to his girlish cousin? Or, to adapt the phraseology of *Jude the Obscure*, was it 'the very unconsciousness of a looming drama' which in retrospect made the Boxing Day visit so impressive? Certainly for Fancy Day and Eustacia the fictional recreation of this visit represents the first move in a time-worn drama.

XVI - ISOLATION AND INEXPERIENCE

Hardy went home. It was the end of July 1865. No doubt he saw from the train window just the parched landscape of that historically exceptional summer that Owen and Cytherea see on their journey down to Dorset after the collapse of Ambrose Graye's architectural practice on a day that is 'one of the most glowing that the climax of a long series of summer heats could evolve.' The anguish of his defeat - if we correctly interpret the journal note of August 1865 - was most fully felt when he had to witness the dismay of his own family. In a calendar of summer 1865 Mrs. Yeobright cannot hide her dismay that Clym has thrown up his job in a great city. In *A Laodicean* the twenty-five year old George Somerset who has recklessly abandoned his dusty drawing-boards is warned by his father that if he does not return to them 'he might have to look elsewhere than at home for an allowance.' For Hardy we may suppose it was a relief to cross the heath and visit Tryphena's home in Puddletown - the 'cheerful house with the sparkling river in front', as Mary Hardy calls it. The hints of the tensions at Bockhampton which Hardy gives in *Life* suggest that at the best of times his own home was never exactly a 'cheerful house'. In some way or other the cousins met. Already there was a certain familiarity. As Millgate aptly observes Hardy could approach the Sparks girls with an ease and informality 'simply because they *were* his cousins.'

The prosaic facts must have been something like this. Perhaps one of the fictions gives a faithful account of the meeting - but I cannot say which, if any. The level of consistency - the level of the covert 1865 calendars, of the formula 'more of a woman in appearance than in years' or of references to Hutchins' *History* - is not that of surface narrative. I could call the method of this sketch dialectical - an arguing out of the conditions that determined the sort of thing that must have happened. The meeting of Pierston with the first Avice makes a good illustration. The narrative may or may not tell us how Hardy met his cousin in 1865 - what we can say is that Avice's discovery of how she has *grown* is a link to the formula 'more of a woman in appearance than in years' and so describes, not the surface event but the deeper, consistent motivation of history repeated through so many of the other fictions.

At this deeper level it seems that it was Hardy's isolation that both drove him from London and also made him capable of becoming a young man. He was that 'isolated student cast upon the billows of London with no protection but his brains.' He would recall the effect of the great city upon him in 'that feeling of gloomy isolation to which young men of Dorset stock are peculiarly liable'. 'The Two Men' of 1866 is explicit about such isolation, but this isolation is also the key to an escape from a habitual repression. Mere consistency points in this direction. There is, for instance, Fitzpiers in the immediate aftermath of Old South's death. Living in 'insulated solitude', as he puts it, he gets 'charged with emotive fluid like a Leyden jar with electric, for want of some conductor at hand to disperse it.' The conductor of this emotional electricity is the Grace Melbury whom Hardy has defined, a page or two before this analysis, as his cousin Tryphena by the reference to her ancestry in the pages of Hutchins' *History* and on the very same page he gives her a whole stanza of Shelley's description of Cythna - the twelve year old mistress of the hero in *The Revolt of Islam*.

Or there is Jude's meeting with the Sue Bridehead who is, as we shall see, connected with Tryphena Sparks by a range of details. At their meeting Jude feels an emotion 'which had been accumulating in his breast as the bottled-up effect of solitude'. Given this characterisation it seems to be no accident that Jude's

Nicholas Hillyard

relationship with his cousin Sue is once more explicitly likened to that of Shelley's Laon and Cythna.[21]

The isolation from which a young man suffers in London is also the key to the hero's entanglement in 'On the Western Circuit', the story Hardy wrote in the autumn of 1891 just before setting to work on *The Well-Beloved*, in which the sunset gnats once more appear to set the calendar in 1865. Raye, the young professional man, comes down from his 'seclusion' in town to seduce a much younger country girl. He supposes

> it must have been owing to the seclusion in which he had lived of late in town that he had given way so unrestrainedly to a passion for an artless creature whose inexperience had, from the first, led her to place herself unreservedly in his hands.

The effects of bottled-up solitude in Fitzpiers or Jude or the hero of 'On the Western Circuit' are wholly consistent with the solitude which forced Hardy to leave London in late July 1865. When he returned home to Bockhampton Tryphena was to make him a *young man* - the effects of solitude seem to have opened

[21] Jude's sexual engagement with Arabella is another version of this biographical moment. His encounter with her on the bank of the stream with the wooden bridge in front of her father's house is an evocation of Tryphena's home in Puddletown. The selection of one girl out of the three on the bank of the stream recalls the Sparks sisters, another of whom - Martha - Hardy is said at one time to have wished to marry. Jude's isolated existence as a student of Greek and theology is broken open by Arabella's attractions, just as Hardy's existence as an isolated student 'reading incessantly' in the summer of 1865 was prelude to 'his development in virility' with Tryphena.

the door to a license Hardy had hitherto been too repressed to exercise.

In these fictional moments Hardy appears to be recalling the predisposing conditions that enabled him to seduce his young cousin when he came home defeated from London. But there is a matching consistency in the picture of the young girl's vulnerabilities. On Hardy's side the tipping point seems encapsulated in the formula 'more of a woman in appearance than in years.' It is a formula which implies the commanding role of sexual appetite in the affair. But it is also an exculpation - it is as if Tryphena's physical development had *deceived* him. But it is the girl's relationship within their extended family and her youthfulness which make her so vulnerable.

Hardy could approach the Sparks girls because they were his cousins. Tryphena was the youngest of them by a margin. She was eight years younger than her nearest brother in age and seventeen years younger than her nearest sister, Martha. Hardy's visit to his aunt in Puddletown in company of his mother in a 'fantastic garb' of cabbage nets may have pre-dated Tryphena's birth, but Tryphena herself must have been familiar with her cousin from earliest childhood. On her side a certain *unreserve* must have been the consequence of that familiarity. This is certainly a topic in the fictions, but as we shall see in a moment it is in fact only an extension of the formula 'more of a woman in appearance than in years'.

The hero of 'On the Western Circuit' recognises that his sexual success is due to the fact that young

Anna is 'an artless creature whose inexperience had, from the first, led her to place herself unreservedly in his hands.' The characterisation is tremendously precise for this sentence is - musically speaking - an inversion of the first insight we are given into young Anna's nature when the narrator calls her - 'Unreserved - too unreserved - by nature, she was not experienced enough to be reserved by art....' *Inexperience* and *unreserve* are traits inextricably bound up with the formula 'more of a woman in appearance than in years' - the formula by which Hardy described what had seemed to him Tryphena's physical precocity at the juncture of 1865.

In *The Well-Beloved* Avice the Third - and Hardy specially inserted the sentence calling her 'more of a woman in appearance than in years' into his 1897 revision - is 'too inexperienced to be reserved'. Geraldine, whose fineness of figure in the calendar of 1865 makes her seem 'more womanly than she really was', is twice described as 'unreserved'. But that, to Hardy's mind, the *unreserve* or *inexperience* are an integral part of the formula 'more of a woman in appearance than in years' is something the manuscript of *Tess* makes clear.

In the second chapter of *Tess* Hardy originally wrote - 'This young girl had an attribute which almost amounted to a disadvantage - emotion unleavened by experience.' But the manuscript shows that he then crossed out the introductory flourish and bodily transferred it to Tess's first meeting with Alec in chapter five where it reads, 'She had an attribute which amounted to a disadvantage just now.....It was a luxuriance of aspect, a fullness of growth, which made her appear more of a woman than she really was.' What the transposition makes clear is that in Hardy's mind the qualities of *inexperience* or *unreserve* are an inseparable connotation of the formula 'more of a woman in appearance than in years'. The girl's appearance and her inexperience conspire together to make her vulnerable.

A further element to add to this complex little bundle of qualities - or exculpations - may well be those 'graces of motion in the body' celebrated by Gray's *Progress of Poesy*. Raye first sees Anna gyrating on a steam roundabout. But the device may be only a cunning disguise for the dance. At each turn of the roundabout Anna and Raye gaze at each other 'with that unmistakeable expression which means so little at the moment, yet so often leads up to passion, heart-ache, union, disunion, devotion, overpopulation....' The Egdon dance which Eustacia attends with Wildeve attracts the same moralisation - 'How many of those impassioned but temporary embraces were destined to become perpetual was possibly the wonder of some of those who indulged in them...' On the roundabout Anna is 'absolutely unconscious of everything save the act of riding: her features were rapt in an ecstatic dreaminess; for the moment she did not know her age or her history or her lineaments, much less her troubles.'[22] At the Egdon dance - 'Eustacia floated round and round.....her face rapt and statuesque; her soul had passed away from and forgotten her features,

---

[22] Compare 'ecstatic dreaminess' with 'It was then that the ecstasy and the dream began' - describing the dance on the eve of Tess's seduction.

which were left empty and quiescent...' The figures on the roundabout move with a 'quiet grace' - Anna herself looks 'so graceful on the horse.' It was such 'graces of motion in the body' which invest the dancing Cytherea with the 'purple light'. Hardy seems to make a private note of the scene's significance when he makes Anna respond to the pleasures of the roundabout 'with dancing eyes'.

The scene at the fair is the prelude to young Anna's seduction. We may speculate that it is a reminiscence of those 'mixed Christmas parties' at which the thirteen year old Cytherea is seen dancing which Hardy associated with his Boxing Day visit to the Sparks in 1864 - a visit which also stands as a prelude in Hardy's mind to his seduction if his young cousin in the ensuing summer. We have at least drawn together a complex of conditions - and these are part exculpation, part objectivity - which account for the central fact of the summer of 1865. They give additional security to the conclusion that Hardy had intercourse with his girl cousin in this summer by making *how* it happened so thoroughly intelligible.

XVII - PORTLAND

A few other parts of the picture may be cautiously restored. For instance, there is a question which has a bearing on this summer, though hitherto it has not seemed to be a question at all. Why did Hardy choose Portland as the scene of his memorial novel to Tryphena? And why was it Portland he actually visited in the wake of Tryphena's death as he makes his hero Pierston do?

Hardy sent the story 'Destiny and a Blue Cloak' to be published in America the week before his marriage to Emma Gifford. As I have shown the story is replete with references to Tryphena and her family. The insistence on these details might tempt us to read 'Destiny and a Blue Cloak' as a despairing last will and testament about Tryphena before marriage closed over Hardy's head. At the beginning of the story Oswald and young Agatha take a trip to Portland by a steamer which 'plowed the emerald waves of Weymouth bay.'

In the end-paper of a French textbook Hardy bought in 1865 and used for the French course he took in the winter of 1865-6, Mariette's *Half-Hours of French Translation*, there are three sketches done from memory - a sketch map of Weymouth and Portland, a view of Portland from the mainland and a rudimentary representation of the cable railway called the Merchant's Incline which carried stone down the steep northern bluff of Portland. The sketches may suggest this was a scene Hardy had recently visited. The summer of 1865 was the last summer he could have visited Portland by steamer as the young principals of 'Destiny and a Blue Cloak' do - the Weymouth and Portland Steam Packet Service ceased trading when the Portland railway opened in the autumn of 1865.[23]

---

[23] The Portland railway was completed by the summer of 1865, but not opened until the autumn due to commercial dispute. In *The Well-Beloved* Hardy may play on this circumstance in having the railway both open and not open in the three parts of the novel which represent the 'same' 1865, just as the three Avices are the 'same' Avice.

The Steam Packet Service was part of a sight-seeing industry attracted by the huge civil-engineering works of the Portland breakwater. Hardy could have got the idea for such a visit from Albert Brett whom he had met on Boxing Day 1864. Brett's diary records making such a trip from Puddletown with a Miss Hibbs in the summer of that year. The Merchant's Incline of Hardy's sketch was a very short walk from the steamer pier at Portland.

Did Hardy set Tryphena's memorial novel *The Well-Beloved* on Portland because he had visited the island with her in the summer of 1865 - the date at which the calendar sets the opening of the novel? There are hints that this was the case. I have cited 'The Musing Maiden' of 1866 as evidence that the scene of the poem was the Ridgeway looking out to Portland. But the maiden's understanding of the Portland quarrying industry - she understands that the distant coasters are carrying Portland stone for the construction of the Thames Embankment - brings into sudden focus the inclusion of that rudimentary sketch of the trucks on the Merchant's Incline in the textbook Hardy was using in the winter of 1865-6. It suggests at the very least an association between this 1866 maiden and Portland itself.

Consistency once again seems to be at work. The sketched view of Portland on the end-paper of the Mariette is from the Ridgeway above Weymouth. This appears to be the 'hog-backed down' of the musing maiden of 1866, just as the Hardy Monument that crowns the Ridgeway appears in the illustration to the maiden's 'She, to Him' sonnets of 1866 in the first edition of *Wessex Poems*. Now it seems that the maiden of these early poems was Tryphena we may give full weight to her friendship with the Spillers at Waddon, a hamlet overlooked by the Hardy Monument, even though the evidence for this friendship dates from no earlier than 1875. This might account for the view of Portland from the mainland - but how about the Merchant's Incline and a visit to Portland itself?

The Well-Beloved carefully imitates that trio of events recorded in *Life* at the time of Tryphena's death. The last of these is the pilgrimage Pierston makes to Portland in the wake of Avice's death. Hardy has identified the death of his fictional heroine with three events from his own life, so that with Pierston's pilgrimage to Portland it is difficult to avoid the feeling that Hardy is here revealing the inner significance of his own visit to Portland at Easter 1890. If this was indeed a memorial pilgrimage like Pierston's - an outing that would have been utterly characteristic of Hardy - it implies an earlier visit to Portland with Tryphena. Such a visit has every appearance of being recorded in the first stanza of 'The Voice of Things'.

There has been casual speculation that the scene of 'The Voice of Things' is set in Cornwall. But, if we are looking for autobiographical veracity, the poem's timetable makes Cornwall impossible. 'The Voice of Things' was printed in 1917 and its three stanzas record three visits to a coastal scene at roughly twenty year intervals. If the scene is set in Cornwall the poem can accommodate Hardy's earliest visits to St. Juliot from 1870. But he did not visit Cornwall once between the time of his marriage to Emma and her death in 1912 nearly forty years later. So a better chronological fit needs to be found. I suggest that the poem was written in 1910 after Hardy's visit to the fleet at Portland. The visit a double decade earlier will be the Portland visit of Easter 1890 recorded in *Life* and that of 'Forty Augusts, aye, and several more ago' a visit of the 1860s. The first stanza's 'loosed from dull employ' would make a succinct reference to Hardy's temporary release by Blomfield in the summer of 1865, while the gloomy mood of the second stanza would fit the possibility that Hardy's visit to Portland at Easter 1890 was prompted by the death of Tryphena - this, in the lightly veiled references of *The Well-Beloved*, is precisely the motive given to Pierston for making his pilgrimage to Portland. The third stanza will then neatly reflect the visit of 1910. If Hardy and his cousin visited Portland by steamer - and in the August of 1865 they would still have been obliged to take the steamer - it readily explains why it was precisely a visit to the fleet at Portland which recalled this long succession of memories.

This dating of the visits of 'The Voice of Things' seems to be confirmed by a poem which Hardy describes as 'Rewritten from an old copy'. This is 'The Wind's Prophecy'. It shares a highly distinctive image with 'The Voice of Things'. 'The Voice of Things' has 'The waves huzza'd like a multitude below', while 'The Wind's Prophecy' has 'The waves outside where breakers are/Huzza like a mad multitude.' Given that 'The Wind's Prophecy' was rewritten from an old copy it looks as though it must be the source of the image in 'The Voice of Things'. But I think we can be more precise about the date of some of the materials of 'The Wind's Prophecy', for this image occurs a third time in *Ethelberta* as 'the waves sending up a sound like the huzzas of multitudes'. This phase of the narrative of *Ethelberta* preserves a matrix of details also found in *The Well-Beloved* - parallels which should point in the direction of a common origin in *The Poor Man*.[24] This would give a date for the huzza'ing waves of some time before the summer of 1867 which would accord well enough with the indication of 'an old copy'.

It only needs a hint that 'the headland vulturine' of 'The Wind's Prophecy' is Portland to make my interpretation of 'The Voice of Things' pretty complete. 'The headland vulturine/Snores like old Skrymer in his sleep.' At the opening of *The Well-Beloved* Portland is described as 'the head of a bird' which has both its 'afternoon sleep' and its 'snores'. But it is the serial version of the novel which makes the identity certain. There Portland had been characterised not as 'the head of a bird' but as 'the head of a flamingo'. The explanation for this curious aviary - neither vulture nor flamingo are Dorset birds! - is that Hardy had consulted his Greek lexicon for the nearest homophones he could find to *Phena*, as he calls his cousin in 'Thoughts of Phena'.[25] In the lexicon he would find both flamingo (*phoenicopterus*) and vulture (*phene*) so that if this is why Portland is flamingo it must certainly be Portland that is also vulture. This

---

[24] A speculation probably confirmed by the occurrence in this matrix in *The Well-Beloved* of the variant description of the sound of waves as 'shouts of thanksgiving'.

[25] See Appendix.

arcane identification with Hardy's cousin now makes full sense of the chronology of 'The Voice of Things'. It anchors the poem's 'Forty Augusts - aye, and several more - ago' in the 1865 when Hardy was temporarily 'loosed from dull employ'.

The symbolism Hardy drew from his lexicon points us to another poem which has every appearance of dramatising what I now take to be an 1865 visit to Portland. This is 'The Place on the Map'. Just as Portland appears to be identified with Tryphena by the Greek homophones for vulture and flamingo, so the 'jutting height' of this poem is 'Coloured purple, with a margin of blue sea.' This purple - found also in 'The Revisitation' - is the 'rare device/Of reds and purples' which is the heart of Hardy's lexical naming of his cousin - Greek *phoenix* being purple-red. This identification with Tryphena makes sense both of the map of the poem and the indication of the subtitle Hardy gave the poem when he first printed it - 'A Poor Schoolmaster's Story'. The map with its 'shires and towns and rivers lined in varnished artistry' which hangs beside the schoolmaster narrator is evidently a school map. I find it difficult to believe that this is not an allusion to the sampler showing the counties of England and Wales which was worked at school by Tryphena and dated 1865. 'Weeks and weeks we had loved beneath that blazing blue' both suggests the meteorology of 1865 and the extended holiday Blomfield had granted Hardy in that year and would naturally explain why Tryphena's sampler came to mind. It even seems that a time around August is suggested. The poem dates its episode to 'latter summer' - an expression which may be compared with 'the later summer-time' which in *Desperate Remedies* indicates August (1865).[26]

There is a further probability. The family tradition that Hardy had undertaken to teach Tryphena French seems to be substantiated by the emphasis placed on the loan of the Stiévenard to Avice III - a heroine identified with Tryphena in being 'more of a woman in appearance than in years' and by her role as the recurrent representative of Hardy's cousin in the structuring of *The Well-Beloved*. If the Stiévenard was lent to Tryphena it seems more than a mere possibility that he also lent her the Mariette, which was the other course book he worked from in the winter of 1865-6. This would explain why he made the sketches of Portland in an end-paper of the book. The sketch at the foot of the page reproduces the view from 'the hog-backed down' of the 1866 poem 'The Musing Maiden'

---

[26] Of course, there are hazards in imputing autobiography to the piece. The fact that it was first printed in 1913 might make a Cornish setting attractive and this was perhaps Millgate's cue for suggesting the poem recalls an episode of 1870 in Hardy and Emma's courtship. *Some* autobiographical significance is surely betrayed by the nature of the revisions Hardy made to the fifth stanza where what would have joyed the lovers' double soul wears a torrid tragic light 'Under order-keeping's rigorous control'. This last phrase had been variously 'superstition's hideous control' or 'merciless control'. These are passionate emendations, but they make no sense in connection with an Emma who wanted and was fully able to marry Hardy. They make every sense in connection with the fourteen year old girl Tryphena was in the summer of 1865. 'Superstition's hideous control' is surely Hardy's shorthand for the negative constraints of religion, a theme that might be investigated with the Sparks and one which looms large in Sue Bridehead's withdrawal from Jude. There is, as Millgate notes, a clear allusion to a real or imagined pregnancy - a hint that should have been taken up by Lois Deacon - indicating that the schoolmaster has had intercourse in the 'blazing blue' hot summer weather.

and it is now clear that the maiden of that poem was Tryphena. The cursory sketch-map of Weymouth and Portland and the sketch of the Merchant's Incline on the same page may now also be seen as having a special significance for Tryphena, if Hardy had indeed loaned her the book, as a record of their recent visit to Portland.

XVIII - THE LETTERS

A mark in his Prayer Book indicates that Hardy was back in London by the second week in September 1865. He had not availed himself of the full nine weeks' holiday Blomfield had offered him. The state of his relations with his young cousin can be inferred from the 'She, to Him' sonnets. Their maiden feels she has been betrayed both by the lover's indifference and, on the evidence of 'She, to Him' IV, by the appearance of a rival. Had Hardy renewed his connection with Eliza Nicholls? In an architectural notebook there is a sketch of the church at Eliza's father's home at Findon made at Whitsun 1866. But the maiden who maledicts this rival is still the inspiration of the whole cycle of sonnets. As to the sonnets themselves it is hard to believe that a certain compunction was not at the root of this large undertaking. The very act of composing the cycle suggests a change of heart from the indifference with which the maiden reproaches the poet to a distinct regret on his part. Somewhere in this obscure emotional realignment is the clue to the fact that the affair was not broken off - to the fact that Hardy was not to have his last interview with Tryphena until July 1870.

If Tryphena communicated with her cousin in the immediate aftermath of his return to London in September 1865 it must have been by letter. How else could the 'rural maid' of 'From Her in the Country' convey her thoughts to her lover in town? The fictions and poems offer suggestive evidence of such a correspondence at just such a date. *An Indiscretion* is quite clear on the matter. It dates the correspondence of the lovers Mayne and Geraldine to the autumn of 1865 after Mayne has gone away to London. But the correspondence is banned by Squire Allenville, the heroine's father, and this is a motif which makes it clear that the novella inherited the lovers' letter-writing from *The Poor Man*. Hardy told Gosse that the Squire of the suppressed novel had forbidden the correspondence of his daughter with the young architect Will Strong, who had also departed for London. It seems to have been a correspondence of precisely the same date as that of *An Indiscretion* since the romance of *The Poor Man* has once more every appearance of being set in a calendar of 1865.

This whole complex of material re-surfaces in *A Pair of Blue Eyes*. Now it is Parson Swancourt who bans Elfride's letter-writing to the young architect Stephen Smith - a Swancourt who inherits the mantle of the Squire of *The Poor Man* since he shares with him both the ban on his daughter's letter-writing and the Squire's town address in Chevron Square. The parson's daughter is now the 'infantine' Elfride who is the child/woman of the novel's 1864/1865 calendar, just as Geraldine is 'such a child' and looks 'more womanly than she really was' in this same calendar of 1865 in *An Indiscretion*.[27]

'Destiny and a Blue Cloak' has its intimate hints of the Sparks household in Puddletown and its heroine is the child/woman Agatha. When young Oswald has departed for India Agatha keeps up a correspondence with him. India had also been Stephen Smith's destination in *A Pair of Blue Eyes*. I take it this southern country is a convenient substitute for London. The motif first occurs in 'The Unplanted Primrose' of 1865-7 when, in a year that is evidently 1865, the neglectful lover departs for 'a southern country'. Hardy dates the poem 1865-7 - a dating which brings us as close as possible to the autumn 1865 date of the lovers' correspondence in *An Indiscretion*.

1865 also seems to offer a convincing context for the letters which feature decisively in the denouement of *The Mayor of Casterbridge*. Lucetta who is the writer of the letters has some tell-tale characteristics. The manuscript shows that Hardy gave special attention to a passage describing her peculiar *flexuousness* which he finally reduced to the sentence - 'Her gait, too, had a flexuousness about it, which seemed to avoid angularity of movement less from choice than from predisposition.' This is very nearly Cytherea Graye's 'flexibility and elasticity' which 'had never been taught her by rule, nor even been acquired by observation, but, *nullo cultu*, had naturally developed itself with her years.' Lucetta defends her 'foolish girl's passion' by

---

[27] See section XXIX below for the logic of the assertion that Stephen and Elfride's correspondence is also dated to the autumn of 1865.

saying 'I was what I call innocent all the time they called me guilty' - an echo of the *pure woman* who is both the 1865 heroine of *An Indiscretion* or the 'Pure Woman' of the title-page of *Tess*. When Henchard admits 'we honestly meant to marry' we gather that Lucetta's reputation is the result of a sexual scandal. Lucetta is also 'well educated' and first thoughts in the manuscript call her 'a good scholar' from 'a good old family, if poor' - this last a suggestion of those musings on his maternal ancestry betrayed by Hardy's underlinings in Hutchins's *History*. These details strongly suggest that behind the writer of the letters lurks the image of Hardy's cousin Tryphena. The narrative context of the letter-writing equally suggests a précis of the year 1865.

Henchard has made one of his trips to Jersey and 'there I fell quite ill, and in my illness I sank into one of those gloomy fits I sometimes suffer from, on account o' the loneliness of my domestic life.' There he meets Lucetta - 'when I was pulled down she took upon herself to nurse me. From that she got to have a foolish liking for me....we got naturally intimate.'[28] It is here that Henchard exonerates himself by saying they had honestly meant to marry - but Lucetta 'was terribly careless of appearances, and I was perhaps more, because o' my dreary state.....At last I was well and came away. When I was gone she suffered much on my

---

[28] If there is a hint here that Tryphena was drawn in by her sympathy for Hardy's illness, it may be paralleled by the scene in *The Return of the Native* where Clym assists in retrieving the lost bucket. Eustacia is betrayed into an anxious solicitude that Clym will fall into the well in a context of the seven men on the rope which seems to allude to the disaster on the Matterhorn.

account, and didn't forget to tell me so in letters one after another.'

Lucetta's flexuousness, the depression related to solitude, the illness, the habitual going to Jersey - a gloss on going home to Bockhampton because, as *Life* tells us, the Hardys are natives of Jersey - and the girl's carelessness of appearances or 'unreserve', as Hardy elsewhere calls it, make a comprehensive adumbration of the events of 1865.[29] It is a story that leads naturally and directly to the writing of the reproachful letters. In Lucetta's flexuousness and in Elfride, Geraldine and young Agatha's child/woman status - all hovering about a calendar of 1865 - we see the young Tryphena of that year. Regularly these heroines are letter writers and what after all could be more natural than that Tryphena should have written to her cousin in the autumn of 1865 when he had returned to Blomfield's office in London?

In March 1890 the theme emerges from the thicket of fictional consistencies into the open - if we may call 'Thoughts of Phena' a candid autobiographical expression. The very opening line of the poem declares 'Not a line of her writing have I', but now it must seem nearer the truth to say that Hardy *no longer* had such writings. As soon as *Tess* was completed the theme of the letters becomes the fulcrum of the plot of 'On the Western Circuit', the story which Hardy wrote in the

---

[29]There may even be an allusion to the Matterhorn since the manuscript shows that Hardy first thought of attributing Henchard's illness to a fall, in which case the manuscript aside 'an account of it was in the papers at the time' may be taken as a reminiscence of the publicity the Matterhorn disaster attracted.

autumn of 1891. As far as this letter-writing goes the short story acts as a little prelude to *The Pursuit of the Well-Beloved* which Hardy began in this same autumn. On the very first page of the novel we see the hero burning old love-letters, one cache of which has every appearance of being Tryphena's. These are the letters of the 'school-girl she'[30] - a girl whom Pierston 'had never much cared for' - and as they catch fire there is a little fizzle and Pierston realises to his horror that he is burning not only the girl's letters but her hair - a detail which makes such a direct connection with the opening of 'Thoughts of Phena' -

> Not a line of her writing have I,
> Not a thread of her hair....

In 'Thoughts of Phena' the poet retains only the girl's phantom as 'relic'. The opening chapter of *The Pursuit of the Well-Beloved* which sees Pierston burning both the schoolgirl's letters and hair is precisely entitled 'Relics' and now that we have shown how the whole novel is constructed around Tryphena's history we may conclude that it must have been in some freak of moral fortitude that Hardy had burned his cousin's letters and a lock of her hair at some time prior to 1890.

---

[30]Tryphena was certainly a schoolgirl in 1865. Hardy even seems to have a particular handwriting in mind. The schoolgirl's 'thick and rotund' handwriting may be compared with that of Ethelberta - 'her strokes were firm, and comparatively thick for a woman's' - who is described as an under-age heiress and, in addition to eyebrows like slurs in music, borrows details of her characterisation from the picture of the Sparks' household in 'Destiny and a Blue Cloak'. Sue Bridehead writes in 'a bold womanly hand' and like Tryphena is both cousin and teacher. Does Hardy know any other kind of female handwriting - apart from the lampoon on Elizabeth-Jane's?

Pierston burns bundles of letters, but only two are described in any detail. One contains those of the schoolgirl. The other is also a bundle of love letters with an equally suggestive history.

> Many of the sentiments, he was ashamed to think, he had availed himself of in some attempts at lyric verse, as having in them that living fire which no lucubration can reach.

Long ago Deacon and Coleman wondered whether this had been Hardy's own practice. This was surely the case. Such an inspiration perfectly accounts for the form the 'She, to Him' sonnets take, speaking as they do in the voice of the maiden and replete with the characteristic exaggerations of love-letters. In one outlier of the cycle - 'From Her in the Country' - the girl finds no solace in the countryside and longs to be with her lover in town - a sentiment which in the mid-Victorian days of the sonnet's composition could only have been conveyed by penny post.[31] The maiden of the sonnets and the Tryphena who wrote to Hardy when he returned to London in the autumn of 1865 were one and the same person. At whatever imaginative remove it seems to have been the *sentiments* of her letters which underpinned the cycle.

---

[31] *An Indiscretion* seems to be aware of the method. At the door of the schoolroom the heiress Geraldine listens to the children reading - the last of them in 'a shrill voice spelling out letter by letter.' It seems, she says, 'quite a little poem.' To which the hero darkly replies, 'Yes...But perhaps, like many poems, it was hard prose to the originators.' In 1978 an early draft of this section was shown to Millgate who found the thesis convincing enough to adapt it to Eliza Nicholls as the inspiration of the 'She, to Him' sonnets in his 1982 biography.

The 'Relics' chapter of *The Pursuit of the Well-Beloved* describes two bundles of letters - those which Pierston had used to inspire his attempts at lyric verse and those of the schoolgirl, including a lock of her hair. But once the minutiae of Hardy's presentation are put under the microscope we may suspect this division is only a disguise which hides their underlying unity. The 'school-girl' had written in a 'thick and rotund hand' and when Pierston finds not just her letters but that her hair is also burning he exclaims - 'I am burning *her* - part of her form - many of whose curves as remembered by me I have worked into statuettes and tried to sell.' Pierston is a sculptor - but his membership of the Academy, with its allusion to the publication of *Desperate Remedies*, is a transparent gloss on Hardy's own career as a novelist and the mask slips a little further in the admission that in his youth Pierston had also resembled Hardy in being a poet. There is here a covert identification of Pierston's career with Hardy's literary career. The 'statuettes' might therefore be glossed as diminutive works of literature. The only such small works which Hardy 'tried to sell' - and failed to sell - were the poems of 1865-7, among them the 'She, to Him' sonnets, which, *Life* tells us, failed to find favour with magazine editors. The 'curves as remembered by me' - such an awkward phrase! - could therefore be the curves of the girl's figure - the realm of the sculptor - or the curves of the girl's 'rotund' handwriting in the letters which were to inspire the poet. In this light the schoolgirl and the writer of the letters which inspired early attempts at lyric verse were one and the same person.

If we step back from these minutiae for a moment it is clear that after the entanglement of the summer of 1865, with its unlooked for development in virility, Hardy tried to retreat from any commitment that entanglement might imply. This is the burden of the maiden's reproach. But authorship is also a definite player in Hardy's retreat from his heady loss of self-control. The creation of the 'She, to Him' sonnets might almost be taken as the moment when authorship claimed its dues in defiance of any happiness Hardy might have achieved as mere man. It seems that Tryphena understood this moment even as it was happening. She wrote to Hardy - this is surely what prompted the 1867 sonnet 'Her Reproach' - that the lure of Fame was destroying 'live love'. Tryphena, as everything we know about her attests, lived in the present in a way that Hardy was totally unequipped to do. His forte is the past of remorse or the day-dreaming anticipation of his 'forefelt wonder of women' - never the present. The condition of being only permitted to love in retrospect is spelt out in Pierston's harrowing confession when he receives the news of the death of the first Avice -

> He loved the woman dead and inaccessible as he had never loved her in life....Yet now the years of youthful friendship with her, in which he had learnt every fibre of her innocent nature, flamed up into a yearning and passionate attachment, embittered by regret beyond words.

This passage is, of course, a blueprint for the poems Hardy was to write at the death of Emma Hardy. It is precisely as Pierston commits the school-girl's letters to his bonfire that we are casually told that 'he had never cared much for her.' With the death of Avice this motif of the lover's indifference rises to an anguished cry - but it is an admission already present in a poem of the mid 1860s in the slighting reference to the young girl as nothing more than 'Maiden meet...till arise my forefelt/Wonder of women.'[32] In 1866 it is also the admission writ large in the 'She, to Him' sonnets which give contemporary witness to Hardy's conflicted and contradictory indifference to Tryphena.

If we are to take that 'yearning and passionate attachment, embittered by regret beyond words' as essentially Hardy's own response to the news of his cousin's death - and the whole construction of *The Well-Beloved* argues that this must certainly have been the case - we can see just why it was that the letters of the fourteen year old Tryphena were the first things to come to mind in March 1890. Even if he had burned them the recollection of them remained an indelible indictment of Hardy's failure to pursue 'live love'. However delusive the retrospect may have been, the bitter regret Pierston or Hardy feels is for his failure to take the path that might have led - not to art, but to emotional fulfillment. The letters come to mind at the moment of Tryphena's death - 'Not a line of her writing have I' as 'Thoughts of Phena' disconsolately puts it. The letters figure prominently at the very threshold of the start of work on Tryphena's memorial novel in the short story 'On the Western Circuit' and it is the ambiguities of this story which seem to give the

---

[32]'The Temporary the All' - a poem Gittings persuasively dates to the mid 1860s. In all probability it was written in the first half of 1867.

clearest insight into what really constituted the tragedy of 1865/6.

The young professional man who has seduced the inexperienced country girl returns to London in a state of confusion. Sometimes he is 'oppressed by absurd fondness for her', but he also hopes her distance from town will 'effectually hinder this summer fancy from greatly encumbering his life.'[33] This is the ambiguity which hovers about the 1865-7 poems. In 'Revulsion' the poet wants to tear the very idea of love out of his heart, but elsewhere the girl is 'the sweetest image outside Paradise'. The same ambiguity hovers about *The Well-Beloved*. When Pierston burns the letters and the hair of the school-girl who had been in love with him we are told that 'he had never much cared for her', but once Avice is dead he cannot help feeling 'a yearning and passionate attachment, embittered by regret beyond words.' 'On the Western Circuit' puts it more prosaically than this in its investigation of the clash of sex and sentiment.

The hero of the story, Raye, shrinks from the simple and impossible young girl with whom he has become entangled through sexual compulsion. But the girl of attractive physicality, seen moving so gracefully on the roundabout at the opening of the tale, seems to have sentiments and a soul as well once the letters written in her name follow Raye back to London. The girl's mistress, Mrs. Harnham, writes these letters on behalf of the illiterate Anna - they contain Mrs.

---

[33] Hardy uses the phrase 'summer fancy' despite the fact that the tale is ostensibly set in the autumn.

Harnham's 'own impassioned pent-up ideas - lowered to monosyllabic phraseology in order to keep up the disguise'. This *impassioned* quality is the same 'living fire' of the letters Hardy was soon to describe at the opening of *The Pursuit of the Well-Beloved*. It is the passionate quality of the prose we can intuit behind such lines as 'This love puts all humanity from me', 'One who would die to spare you touch of ill,' or 'I will be faithful to thee; aye, I will!' - lines which might be picked almost at random from the densely packed sentiments of the four surviving 'She, to Him' sonnets. These formulations are drawn from the prose of Tryphena's letters of the fall of 1865 and the letters seem to have revealed a range of emotion Hardy could scarcely have anticipated when he had intercourse with a young girl he had only known through the frame of familiarity as the youngest of his Puddletown cousins. This would seem to be the autobiographical point of 'On the Western Circuit'.

Beneath the surface simple Anna and impassioned Mrs. Harnham are two faces of a single original. This is no doubt why Hardy made a late addition to the tale of the improbable device of making Raye take Mrs. Harnham's hand in the crowd under the illusion that it is Anna's. Even without this motif the narrative keeps hinting at the essential identity of the two - Mrs. Harnham is 'little less impulsive than Anna herself' or 'almost as unaccustomed as the maiden herself to the end-of-the-age young man.' At the close of the story it is not Anna's body, but Mrs. Harham's sentiments conveyed in the letters which induce Raye to do the decent thing and marry the girl. The last twist of the tale is the revelation that the letter-writer is not the maid but the mistress - Raye is obliged to accept his marriage to his 'unlettered peasant' with 'dreary resignation'. The hero's queasiness at this denouement can be traced all the way back to 1866 - the date of that dark poem 'To a Bridegroom' which simultaneously exposes the dread of marriage and the poet's conflicted attitude to the girl's physical attractions.

Despite the accusation of abandonment voiced in the 'She, to Him' sonnets the affair somehow persisted. Hardy was not to have his final interview with Tryphena until the July of 1870. The letters may have been a turning point in Hardy's perceptions of his cousin, but these were only complicating perceptions. Hardy could not overcome the solitary temptation to use or abuse the letters as so much grist for conversion into poetry. Hardy may have known that the 'dead page' of literary pursuit was incompatible with 'live love' - and Pierston may have been *ashamed* that he had turned a girl's love-letters into verse - but it was a conversion Hardy could not help making. Even in the act of pursuing Tryphena he was escaping from her through his art. 'Con the dead page as 'twere live love: press on!' That is how the 1867 sonnet 'Her Reproach' opens. The real intuition of the line lies in the words 'press on!' Hardy was always *pressing on* - with his poems, with *The Poor Man*, with *Desperate Remedies*. Later I shall argue that he presented both these novels as inducements to Tryphena, the first in 1868 and the second in 1870, in willful disregard of the fact that she found his art an alienation. Hardy would press on - trying to have his cake and eat it - disregarding the stark either/or with which the Tryphena of 'Her Reproach' had challenged him.

The correspondence must have begun in September 1865. It probably continued at least as far as the January of the next year. 'Destiny and a Blue Cloak' gives an idea of the contents of the letters Agatha writes to Oswald in the wake of her seduction as a young girl. Among other details the letters had mentioned 'the arrival and departure of birds of passage, the times of storms and foul weather.' This juxtaposition may explain the fact that the gaunt, spectral birds, which arrive at Flintcomb-Ash driven in front of the north wind, are very precisely anticipated by the wild mallard which Venn sees on Egdon in *The Return of the Native*. The inflated evocation of 'glacial catastrophes' in polar regions is extraordinarily similar in these two contexts. In *Tess* the emphatic statement that the birds have kept ahead of the violent snowstorm from the north which eventually reaches Flintcomb-Ash may well have been prompted by the ferocious snowstorm of January 10/11 1866. The *Dorset County Chronicle* reported that 'Large flocks of wild ducks, teal, and widgeon hovered about on the Surrey side of the Thames as if driven by the stress of weather, ultimately flying off towards the south coast.' In Puddletown itself, in addition to the heavy snow, Tryphena could have witnessed trees uprooted and chimneys blown down.

XIX - AN ENGAGEMENT

When we look at the likelihood of an engagement in 1866, the evidence throws up just that sort of ambiguity in Hardy's feelings which is so clear in the whole of his poetic venture of 1865-67. Such an ambivalence towards young women seems typical of the Hardy who had just become a young man. Retrospectively he recalls such uncertainty in his relations with Louisa Harding - an 'attachment' which a cancelled indication in *Life* tells us lasted till his twenty-third or fourth year. In the poem 'The Passer-By' Louisa is made to imagine a rival suffering her own fate - 'He'll make her feel him dear.... Then tire him of her beauteous gear.' To judge by the opening of 'She, to Him' I this was the fate Tryphena also feared - 'When you shall see me in the toils of Time,/My lauded beauties carried off from me.' As an affianced young man the ambiguous note is again sounded in early 1871 when Hardy speaks of himself as 'virtually if not distinctly engaged to be married' to Emma Gifford. He was practiced at creating illusions where young women were concerned.

Hardy may have been the victim of his own illusions. He may have persuaded himself it was just too difficult to choose. To judge by dates Louisa would seem to have been a Dorset rival to Eliza Nicholls. In the hidden recesses of his imagination - as the workings of *A Pair of Blue Eyes* or *The Well-Beloved* show - Tryphena persisted in being one of the more potent rivals of Emma Hardy. The Tryphena of 'She, to Him' IV has a rival of her own, whom she can only 'maledict' and 'pray her dead'.

Was this Eliza Nicholls, with whom Hardy had become familiar in 1863, but who had gone to work in Surrey later that year and, according to Millgate, returned home to live with her parents at Findon near Brighton in January 1865? There is a thumbnail sketch of the church at Findon in Hardy's *Architectural Notebook* dated Whitsun 1866. The church is described as 'near the Downs', but as Millgate records 'the erased word 'Findon' is still faintly discernible.' Hardy is evidently covering his tracks. But the same might be said of the emendations to the sketches he made in the end-papers of his copy of Mariettes's *Half-Hours of French Translation*. At some point he has returned to his sketch-map of Weymouth and Portland and continued the coastline eastwards, starting with Kimmeridge Bay, in a style completely at odds with the cursory strokes of the original - now with the evident assistance of some printed map. This is an *erasure* of a different kind - an erasure of significance, apparently - but a clue to it may be found in yet another sketch in the end-papers of the Mariette in what seems an even more cursory doodle of Clavel Tower which stands on the cliffs by Kimmeridge which was Eliza's childhood home. Below the picture Hardy has written the words 'Devotion' and 'Stoicism'. The words seem to accord well enough with Millgate's picture of Eliza as a woman who 'had never married, never discarded Hardy's ring or portrait.' If this is true, there seems to have been another ring in existence.

There is no good reason to doubt that Hardy and Tryphena had at some period considered themselves engaged. Tryphena's daughter, Mrs. Bromell, asserted that Hardy had been engaged to her mother for five years and recalled that he had given her a ring. The span of five years fits temptingly between 1865 and the parting of July 1870, though Tryphena cannot actually have returned Hardy's ring until after she was ensconced in Plymouth in 1872 since her future husband, Charles Gale, had seen it. Mrs. Bromell could scarcely have been more circumstantial about what her father, Charles Gale, had told her about his insistence on persuading Tryphena to break off her engagement. He does not appear to have been over-fond of Hardy's memory, but he remembered the ring - 'It isn't much of a ring,' he had told his wife to be. Millgate likes to say there was 'probably no formal engagement' between Hardy and his cousin, but he does not contest the existence of the ring and what other significance the ring can have had is hard to see. In Mrs. Bromell's recollections there is a natural and unquestioned connection between the ring and the engagement.[34]

There seems, moreover, to be evidence of a wish to become engaged at precisely the date we must now expect it. In conversation with Vere Collins Hardy explained the 'evergreen nesting-tree' of the 1866 poem 'Postponement' as 'enough money to marry on' - a gloss which invites us to read the poem as an allegory of Hardy's wish, but practical inability to get married at this time. His plan of the same year to secure a country curacy by going up to Cambridge may also have been connected with such practicalities. Even more suggestive evidence for an engagement comes from the unpublished 1866 poem 'To a Bridegroom'.

---

[34] Hardy's secretary was to recall that Emma Gifford was said to have been given a ring that had been intended for a Dorset girl.

Eight intensely gloomy stanzas of this poem survive - there were more, for the MS. describes the poem as 'abridged'. Each stanza presents the case against the bridegroom's putative bride. Her looks may fade, despite her looks she may have no great gifts, she may become an invalid, her hair may thin, a 'tale that wronged her fame' may get out, her love may prove too headstrong. It looks very much like the projection of an argument Hardy is having with himself. Why should he have entertained such a cruelly detailed fantasy if he himself were not fearful of the thought of marriage at this time? The prospective bride has such a definite character it is hard to believe the poet's argument is mere abstraction. There is even a hint of the youthfulness of the girl in the line 'Think her little fingers rough'.

The Poor Man may also have taken a fictive look at the engagement. In his lifetime Hardy acknowledged only a single scene from the book. This was in the poem 'A Poor Man and a Lady' which was 'intended to preserve an episode in the story of 'The Poor Man and the Lady'.' The episode he chose to preserve is rooted in a scene where the lovers secretly engage themselves to be married or perhaps conduct their own marriage ceremony when the man 'placed the ring/On your pale slim hand.' Was this the ring which according to Charles Gale was not much of a ring? Tryphena, of course, was still a young girl. In the March of 1866 she was just fifteen and only just sixteen at the time Hardy began to write *The Poor Man*. Any open engagement must have been out of the question - even discounting the family tradition that Maria Sparks had 'put a spoke' in Hardy's wheel when he wanted to marry Tryphena. Just here, though, the details of the poem 'A Poor Man and Lady' may come to our rescue. Whatever the exact nature of the moment when the Poor Man places the ring on the Lady's pale slim hand, it inaugurates 'a time of timorous secret bliss'. Their engagement is something 'unviewed' by the world - indeed, according to Mrs. Bromell, it was not until her mother left Stockwell College that she began to wear Hardy's ring openly.[35]

There is also the clear implication of an engagement in the 1869 poem 'Singing Lovers' where, as we shall see, there is compelling evidence that it is Tryphena who is 'she of a bygone vow'.

XX - TRUTH AND LIGHT

It is easy enough to gather a number of Hardy's concerns in 1866, but it is difficult to arrange them in a sequence that would make a narrative. In *Life* Hardy

---

[35] In *Desperate Remedies* part of 'Her Dilemma' is prosed into the scene where Cytherea finally capitulates to Manston's proposal of marriage. Apart from the reference to Hardy's 1865 illness an autobiographical significance for the poem seems to be implied by the numerological puzzle incorporated in the illustration provided for it in the first edition of *Wessex Poems*. If the box pews are first counted, then the standing figures and the poppy-headed pews, then the coffins beneath the floor, it is clear the whole illustration spells out the date 1866. An extra refinement may be the boldly asymmetrical presentation of two and a half bays of the church arcade and the fourteen skulls to represent Hardy and Tryphena's respective ages of twenty-five and fourteen - in which case the scene reflects an event of 1866 prior to the March of Tryphena's fifteenth birthday. Did Hardy prose the poem into the scene in which Cytherea becomes engaged to Manston because the poem reflected his own engagement to Tryphena? In that case a rationale for the numerology of the illustration becomes intelligible.

tells us he resumed writing verse in 1865, though no poem indisputably belongs to this year.[36] The fictions suggest that Tryphena began writing to Hardy when he returned to London in the September of 1865, but it is impossible to say at what time in 1866 Hardy began finding in her letters the 'living fire' which inspired his sonnet cycle. 'Her Definition' is dated 'Summer: 1866' and 'The Musing Maiden' 'October 1866', but it is not clear that these dates are anything more than dates of composition. The Whitsun dating of the little sketch of Findon church suggests that Hardy visited Eliza there in the second half of May. There are other important schemes of this year, but we cannot place them exactly. Where are we to date the cousin's engagement and, in the light of the rival of 'She, to Him' IV, was there some rapprochement here? There must have been a 'story', but it is best not to construct too exact a narrative because we will probably get it wrong.

One significant scheme to add to the doings of this year was Hardy's abortive plan to enter the Church. He felt life as a curate in a country village would sit better with poetry than his work as an architect's assistant. After his debility in London it was perhaps the pure country air that appealed to Hardy. That it was a scheme of 1866 is confirmed by the date Hardy's sister Mary gives to his letter describing the insuperable difficulties of time and money which thwarted it. The scheme only seems to belong to 1865 in the narrative of *Life* because of Hardy's cavalier editing. Originally the reference to it had its proper place in 1866. But that was

---

[36] 'Discouragement' is dated 1863-7, but the MS. gives '1865-7'. 'Amabel is dated 1865, but MS. and *Selected Poems* give '1866'.

before Hardy decided to add a number of journal notes of 1865 to his text, which are crowded into the margins of the typescript and clumsily cobbled into the story with an 'About this time...' which makes it appear the scheme belonged to 1865. A note for July 1865 which already stood in the text describes Hardy at work on Newman's *Apologia*, but its amused skepticism - 'Poor Newman! His gentle childish faith in revelation and tradition must have made him a very charming character.' - makes one wonder why Hardy envisaged his Church plan at all. In *Life* he tells us that he 'allowed the curious scheme to drift out of sight' not because of its financial difficulty but 'from a conscientious feeling, after some theological study, that he could hardly take the step with honour while holding the views that on examination he found himself to hold.' This lofty explanation is rather shaken by the plain statement of his contemporary letter to Mary that he had given up the scheme 'on adding up expenses and taking into consideration the time I should have to wait...'.

It is possible that the Church scheme is referred to in both 'The Temporary the All' and in 'The Two Men' of 1866. In the first the poet will make high-handiwork his life-deed - 'Truth and Light outshow'. In 'The Two Men' one of the poem's dual personae will 'brace to higher aims....I'll further Truth and Purity;/Thereby to mend the mortal lot.' The scene of such high thinking is to be 'a visioned hermitage' or a dwelling 'in some dim dell'. Whatever the exact nature of the idealistic plans of the poems, they appear to be referred to in *The Return of the Native* in the summer

1865 of its calendar in Clym's plan to open a school 'to benefit his fellow creatures'. With such work to do he 'could live and die in a hermitage' on Egdon Heath.[37] There was to be no such escape for Hardy. In September 1865, after sufficient recuperation, he had resumed his work at Blomfield's drawing-boards. In his lodgings on the top floor of 16 Westbourne Park Villas he had begun to write poetry. Rather than a scheme to mend the mortal lot, this verse writing is better described by the journal note of 1866 - 'A certain man: He creeps away to a meeting with his own sensations.'

XXI - ELECTIVE ISOLATION

The poems of 1865-7 point to the fact of Hardy's affair of 1865, but they reveal less about the affair itself than his own confusion. In this they corroborate the hints of fictions like 'On the Western Circuit'. Hardy says in *Life* that in 1865 he had begun to write verses again for the first time since he had come to London. Of this period he also says, 'A sense of the truth of poetry, of its supreme place in literature, had awakened itself in me. At the risk of ruining all my worldly

---

[37] In the wake of completing *The Return of the Native* Egbert Mayne appears as a poor schoolmaster in *An Indiscretion*. In the subtitle to the first printing of 'The Place on the Map', a poem which has every appearance of referring to the Portland visit of 1865, the persona was 'A Poor Schoolmaster'. Is this theme merely a fictional transformation of the Church scheme or a hint of an alternative occupation Hardy may have mooted in 1865-6? Given the detailed affinities of Sue Bridehead with Typhena, there can be little doubt that Hardy retrospectively imagined what it might have been like to run a school with his cousin's assistance. In the case of Phillotson - and, indeed, of Clym Yeobright - he does not seem to have imagined the results would have been very brilliant. Was this already a scheme of 1866?

prospects I dabbled in it.....All was of the nature of being led by a mood, without foresight or regard to whither it led.' Such a note of inflation appears in the poems of 1865-7 themselves - in 'A Young Man's Exhortation' or 'The Two Men'. But it was not always a question of rapturous inspiration. There is evidence of hard graft and a return to the late night habits associated with Hardy's depression.

> I lingered through the night to break of day,
> Nor once did sleep extend a wing to me,
> Intently busy with a vast array
> Of epithets that should outfigure thee.

The only result of this midnight lucubration recorded in 'Her Definition' is the words "That maiden mine!" - not a very substantial poetic return.

The sonnet 'Revulsion' emerges from exactly the same setting - but the mood into which it veers away is anything but blissful. Here is the opening quatrain as Hardy originally wrote it.

> Though I waste watches framing words to fetter
> Some own spirit to mine in clasp and kiss,
> Out of the night there looms a sense 'twere better
> To fail obtaining whom one fails to miss.

The instinct is to write - it is almost writing in search of a feeling and as such virtually an admission of bad faith. Hardy is sitting up late trying to write a poem which will fix the feeling of holding and kissing the girl. But there is the looming sense that it might be better to do without this mental clasping or 'obtaining' because he doesn't care for her enough to miss her.

The premise is depressing, but Hardy does not seem to recognise the admission he has made - an upsurge of emotion covers his tracks. He draws a fund of bitterness from the self-evident proposition that 'winning love we win the risk of losing' and the sestet moves rapidly on to the conclusion 'Let me then no more feel the fateful thrilling / That devastates the love-worn wooer's frame.' But is the poet a lover? Is he a wooer? How does this square with the fact that he 'fails to miss' the girl? Re-reading the opening quatrain it is almost as if it is the frustration of being unable to write - the wasting watches - that engenders the destructive emotions of the sonnet's ending - the *revulsion* of the title. The poem shows both why Hardy was lonely and how he was lonely.

The unpleasantness of the sonnet's conclusion only seems to have struck Hardy when he was preparing the poem for publication over thirty years later. He then tried to expunge the disagreeable admission that he was attempting to write a love-poem for a girl he did not really care for. The manuscript shows that he changed the 'own spirit' of the second line to 'unknown spirit' - though it is a little difficult to see how he could fail to miss someone he had never known. Evidently the 'own spirit' of the original was a particular girl and this is why in the sestet Hardy had originally written 'Let me no more feel the fateful thrilling'. So here he was obliged to make another revision. 'No more' clearly implies he definitely *had* been in love - while the 'never' that replaces it reduces the whole argument to an abstract possibility. We can see how Tryphena's letters, which had in them 'that living fire which no lucubration can reach', were a gift for the man who wasted watches trying to write about feelings he himself was uncertain about having.

Tryphena did not need to go into such minutiae of analysis. She understood the destructive effects of Hardy's ambition to be an author - a lesson Emma Gifford had to learn the hard way. In 'Her Reproach' it is presumably the burden of one of her letters that lies behind this outlier of the 'She, to Him' sonnets.

> Con the dead page as 'twere live love: press on!
> Cold wisdom's words will ease thy track for thee;
> Aye, go; cast off sweet ways, and leave me wan
> To biting blasts that are intent on me.
>
> But if thy object Fame's far summits be,
> Whose inclines many a skeleton overlies
> That missed both dream and substance, stop and see
> How absence wears these cheeks and dims these eyes!

In a spirit of irony or bitterness Hardy paraphrases these lines at the beginning of the second part of *An Indiscretion* where he gives a précis of his own literary beginnings and an account of the hero's dismay that they are not a sufficient argument to win back the heiress of the title.[38]

---

[38] There is surely a lingering frisson of the Matterhorn disaster in the summits and the skeletons. There is also that doublet from *Desperate Remedies* and *An Indiscretion* - 'The truly great stand on no middling ledge; they are either famous or unknown.' The haunting recollection of the Matterhorn never seems to have left Hardy. In 1906 he recalled seeing John Stuart Mill on the hustings in the summer of 1865 with the

It was perhaps a mercy that Tryphena could interpret Hardy's indifference as ambition, for the poems of 1865-7 betray a crueler animus against her. Hardy's desire cannot grant her the independence of a separate being. In 'Revulsion' he is attempting to *fetter* her to him. Even in 'Her Definition' the blissful words "That maiden mine!" are likened to a chest 'encasing' the sentiment - indeed, when such chests are 'borne with tenderness through halls of state' they might almost seem to be coffins. But it is the poem 'Heiress and Architect', written some time in the first half of 1867, in which the coffin becomes an actuality. We cannot forget that Hardy himself was an architect who had spent the previous year amassing his sonnet cycle for a maiden. The heiress - she is a 'maid' - comes to the architect to design her halls whose tracery will be open to the scents and sights of nature. The architect rejects such a scheme. The heiress concedes a degree of enclosure - 'wide fronts of crystal glass' - a transparency which will disclose her laughter and her light. But the architect will have none of it - 'Those house them best who house for secrecy.' Now the maid pleads for a little chamber 'with rare device/Of reds and purples' where she can meet her lover. Such a chamber will be intolerable when the lover has betrayed her, the architect warns. Cornered, her last plea is for a winding turret 'To reach a loft where I may grieve alone!' No, says the architect -

> "Give space (since life ends unawares)
> To hale a coffined corpse adown the stairs;

---

suggestive detail that 'his vast pale brow....sloped back like a stretching upland, and conveyed to the observer a curious sense of perilous exposure.'

For you will die."

This murderous attack has a sexual meaning. 'Heiress and Architect' is not the only poem of 1865-7 to confine its heroine to the sepulchral. The opening stanza of the 1866 'To a Bridegroom' performs this imaginative task with extraordinary economy.

> Swear to love and cherish her?
> She might moan were beauty's throne
> Beauty's sepulchre.

With an unconscious rapidity of association the young man passes from the marriage vows, to beauty, to death. The throne of beauty is the outward manifestation of the girl as she is now - the body that will become a sepulchre when she becomes a corpse. There is a carnality here which makes 'beauty' translate as sexual appeal - a meaning borne out by the anxious debate of the body of the poem between the attractions of the girl's silk dress and hair and little fingers as they are now and the ruin of what they are to be.[39]

This sexual morbidity is not an isolated aberration. It can be found elsewhere in early Hardy. There is the opening of *An Indiscretion* where the face of the young heiress is assimilated to the marble skull over her pew in the 'half-dreamy' fancy of the hero. That this is an erotic fantasy is made clear by the epigraph from Shakespeare quoting Angelo's libidinous thoughts in church at the sight of Isabella. In *Desperate Remedies*, in

---

[39] The 'ruined hues' of 'Amabel' - dated to 1866 in MS. and *Selected Poems* - are as likely to be this kind of *future projection* as the evidence of experience that Millgate suggests in proposing the ageing Mrs. Martin as the original of Amabel.

what is evidently a prosing of a version of the lyric '1967', Manston explains how he can only cope with the arousal Cytherea's physical charms cause him by imagining her as a corpse - he feels 'better and sounder' after this contemplation.

In his 'lateness of development in virility' the phase that Hardy calls his *youth* was inaugurated by the most drastic example of this linkage between sexual arousal and violence or death. He became that youth at the age of sixteen. The hanging of Martha Browne which he witnessed took place in August 1856, barely two months after his sixteenth birthday. Much later he was to write, 'what a fine figure she showed against the sky as she hung in the misty rain, & how the tight black silk gown set off her shape as she wheeled half-round & back.' Gittings rightly calls them 'words whose unconscious tone is barely credible' and Millgate refers to the 'strong sexual component' in Hardy's response.

How deeply - and unconsciously - such responses entered into Hardy's soul can be seen from the poem he wrote in celebration of Elizabeth Bishop, the pretty gamekeeper's daughter who, as *Life* tells us, won Hardy's boyish admiration 'because of her beautiful bay-red hair.' It was not just her hair that Hardy admired. In her poetic incarnation she also has 'flesh so fair/Bred out of doors'. But as *Life* tells us, 'she despised him, as being two or three years her junior, and married early.' Hardy entitles his celebration of her 'To Lizbie Browne' and repeats the name no fewer than eighteen times in the course of the poem. It is - even to the final 'e' - the name of the woman he had seen hanged when he was just sixteen years old. This woman is conventionally called Martha Browne so that we forget that her full name was Elizabeth Martha Browne.

This sexual morbidity must surely have a bearing on Hardy's instinct to escape from his young cousin - or from Louisa Harding or any of the longer list of young women connected with his name. It is precisely when he is brought to bay with serious thoughts of marriage that he must think of beauty's throne as beauty's sepulchre. There seems something quite involuntary in the knotty compression of this image that opens the meditation of the 1866 'To a Bridegroom'.

Such destructive feelings may ultimately account for the failure of the cousins' engagement. But it is difficult to draw a simple outline of the affair. In the 'She, to Him' sonnets of 1866 the maiden speaks of herself as one betrayed. On the other hand 'Her Definition' with its cry of "That maiden mine!" is dated to the summer of 1866. But rather than construct a little chronology out of this sudden lift of the spirits it is perhaps just as reasonable to suppose that Hardy, on the deep grounds of the psychology I have sketched out, would at best be an unpredictable lover. Whatever the fortunes of the affair through 1865 and 1866 the first half of 1867 sees the graph descending. 'Neutral Tones', written like all the 1867 poems at Westbourne Park Villas and therefore dating to some time before the end of the July 1867 when Hardy went home to Dorset, imagines - or records - a meeting which only exacerbates the failure of an affair.[40] But it is 'Heiress and Architect' with its murderous negativity which must give the clearest insight into Hardy's mood at the moment he turned from verse to prose. The principals of *The Poor Man and the Lady* were precisely an heiress and an architect and just as the heiress of the poem is immured in a space just big enough to hale her coffin down the stairs, so the fable of the new novel was to end with the Lady's death. There is a rather depressing congruity in all this.

XXII - THE POOR MAN AS A SORT OF REVENGE

Prose has a different meaning from verse. Hardy's career as a novelist more or less coincides with his existence as a 'young man' from the age of twenty-five to 'nearly fifty'. It fits pretty exactly if we take seriously Hardy's comment on *Tess* - the novel he completed in his fiftieth year - that it marked 'the beginning of the end of his career as a novelist.' At the denouement of *The Well-Beloved* the 'curse' of being a 'young man' is removed, but the loss of young manhood and of the

---

[40] 'Neutral Tones' is surely the poem referred to in *Ethelberta* as 'Cancelled Words' - its association with a pond and a conversation in which the hopes of former lovers lose ground, as well as its status as the outstanding poem of the collection called 'Metres by Me' all point to this identification. Retrospectively, then, the principals who meet beside the pond of the novel - Christopher (a name Hardy said he would have preferred to Thomas) as the impractical artist and Ethelberta who is linked with Tryphena by carrying over a number of the allusions from 'Destiny and a Blue Cloak' - may confirm the sense that 'Neutral Tones' is in some sense a 'record' of a moment in the cousins' affair. See below for the connections of Ethelberta's literary career with Hardy's and Appendix for a possible rationale for the 'gray' symbolism of 'Neutral Tones'.

novelist's inspiration are simultaneous and inextricably linked. *Young manhood* - in Hardy's peculiar sense of the term - had been the era of prose. It seems almost to have been a state which put a ban on the writing of poetry.

If the maiden - Tryphena - was a traditional muse, her symbolic destruction in 'Heiress and Architect' must signal the end, however temporarily, of Hardy the poet. There is the tantalising statement of the poem 'After Reading Psalms XXXIX., XL., etc.' which Hardy dates '187-' - 'When I failed at fervid rhymes'. I am tempted to see such a failure in the transition from the verse of 'Heiress and Architect' to the prose of *The Poor Man and the Lady*. There is an account of the genesis of *The Poor Man* given under the disguise of Ethelberta's literary career in *The Hand of Ethelberta*. Ethelberta's prose story is 'written in the first person' and its style is 'modelled after De Foe's' - an exact anticipation of what Hardy tells us about his suppressed first novel in *Life*. It also succeeds the writing of poetry. Ethelberta explains that before taking up this prose story she had become incapable of writing poetry - 'I cannot write a line of verse. And yet the others flowed from my heart like a stream.' Does this admission reflect Hardy's own motives for turning to prose? Does it reflect the 'When I failed at fervid rhymes' of 'After Reading Psalms XXXIX., XL., etc.'?

The truth of the matter is probably encapsulated in the change Hardy made to his title for *The Poor Man*. At first it was to be a story 'Containing some original verses', but Hardy 'ultimately' removed this indication. The incorporated verses must have had some function in the narrative, so that their removal would necessitate their replacement by an equivalent prose and this, it is tempting to think, is the origin of those *prosed* versions of poems of 1865-7 - at least half a dozen of them - which found their way into the text of *Desperate Remedies*.[41] But their transposition into prose - surely an act of vandalism - or their mere removal seems to imply Hardy's disenchantment with the role of poet. What price now of that 'sense of the truth of poetry, of its supreme place in literature'!

Hardy's verse could never have been a livelihood. He claims to have sent the poems of 1865-7 to magazines whose editors did not like them. Then, in the summer of 1867, he tells us 'Almost suddenly he became more practical' and this was his cue for the shift to prose, starting work on *The Poor Man*. His account is very much simplified. He may gloss this momentous development as a matter of practicality - and one of the spurs to such practicality may have been the wish enshrined in the 1866 'Postponement' of 'enough money to marry on'. But I have already argued that Hardy had begun the book by at least the spring of 1867 and it was this that determined his plan to return home to Dorset - a plan already mooted prior to Moule's letter of June 1867 and one which was carried out towards the end of July 1867. The world of self-doubt and emotional ambiguity which the 1865-7

---

[41] The matter would be clinched if a prosing occurred as a doublet. The sentence beginning 'But you will never realise that an incident which filled but a degree in the circle of your thoughts...' in *Two on a Tower*, chapter VI looks precisely like a doublet of the prosing of 'She, to Him' II in *Desperate Remedies* XIII, 4.

poems represent seems suddenly to have been shut off in favour of one of hideous certainty. In *The Poor Man* negative emotions were externalised in a sweeping satire that made one of the novel's few readers feel it inconceivable that so big a cast of characters 'could be so bad without going to utter wreck in a week.'

The Poor Man certainly looks different from the work Hardy was to publish subsequently as the Wessex Novels. Our knowledge of the book largely derives from the surviving correspondence with Macmillan and his reader's report and from two accounts by Hardy - one in the pages of *Life* and one given to Edmund Gosse. Macmillan and his reader have a good deal to say about the *mischief* of the novel's social satire - it made them nervous - and this is the side of the book Hardy emphasises in his account in *Life*. But we have only to compare this account with the details he gave to Gosse - or, indeed, to consider the title *The Poor Man and the Lady* - to see that the presentation of the book in *Life* is designed to obliterate the romantic interest which was at the heart of it. To Gosse Hardy spoke of the book almost wholly in terms of the romance of its two principal characters. He went as far as to say, 'The only interesting thing about it was that it showed a wonderful insight into female character. I don't know how that came about!' In this interest the book was already like its published successors - indeed, in certain moments indistinguishable from those successors in the doublets which enable us to glimpse fragments of the text of *The Poor Man* directly. A number of these doublets - among them the sunset gnats - are implicated in the romance of the principals.

But any attempt to speculate on the autobiographical meaning of the suppressed novel should take both its satire and its romance into account. The doublets - especially one which seems to evoke the physical appearance of Tryphena, of which more in a moment - and the presumption that *The Poor Man* was based on a calendar for 1865 are strong arguments that the book already drew its inspiration from the affair which continues to be a central point of reference for the later novels. Even Hardy's debility of the summer of 1865 seems to have featured in its narrative.[42] But what induced Hardy to lace this narrative with a kind of satire that seems foreign both to the romances of the later Wessex Novels and to the vexed inner world of 'Revulsion' or the 'She, to Him' sonnets?

Between the poems and the start of work on *The Poor Man* something had changed - or perhaps the poem 'Heiress and Architect' heralds the transition, providing as it does a sort of blue-print for the novel with its heiress and its architect. Nathaniel Sparks Jnr. records the tradition that when Hardy wanted to marry Tryphena her mother, Maria Sparks, had 'put a spoke in his wheel'. It may be with such external opposition Hardy did not need to face his inner confusion, but could boldly attack a world which had excluded him. At least, the fable of *The Poor Man* fits such a hypothesis rather neatly.

There are the hints of the 1865-7 poems that Hardy wished to become engaged. There is the special preservation of the secret engagement which was

---

[42] See note 8 above.

evidently a cardinal scene in *The Poor Man*. There is the family tradition that Hardy's attempt to marry Tryphena was foiled by her mother. If Maria Sparks did put a spoke in Hardy's wheel when he wanted to marry Tryphena it must have been before the autumn of 1868, for she died in that September. The manuscript of *The Poor Man* had already been packed off to the publishers at the end of July 1868. Its plot turned about the parental opposition of the Lady's family to the suit of the Poor Man. Such a concatenation of circumstances makes it tempting to view the plot of *The Poor Man* as some sort of dramatisation of the opposition of Tryphena's parents to Hardy's pursuit of their youngest daughter. A number of details suggest that *The Poor Man* was always a novel about the Sparks and about Tryphena in particular.

There is the calendar. It looks as if this first novel initiated the 1865 setting which is obsessively repeated in later fictions. *An Indiscretion*, which relies so heavily on *The Poor Man*, opens with a Christmas scene just as the lost novel did. In the novella this Christmas scene is dated to Christmas 1864. The sunset gnats, drawn as a doublet from the text of *The Poor Man* recur in a context of 1865 in the calendars of both *Desperate Remedies* and *The Return of the Native*. Then there is Tryphena herself. Fancy Day is given Tryphena's profession - even to the unexpected detail of gaining a Queen's Scholarship - the eyebrows like two slurs in music and a brunette beauty which, as Gitings says, 'certainly corresponds in general with photographs of Tryphena.' But Fancy undoubtedly inherits her looks from the Lady of *The Poor Man*. Scattered through the first two chapters of Part the Third in *Under the Greenwood Tree* are little snippets of description of Fancy - 'An easy bend of the neck and graceful set of the head; full and wavy bundles of dark-brown hair; light fall of little feet...clear deep eyes...[her cheek's] varying tones of red...the ripe tint of her delicate mouth.' Each of these phrases reappears verbatim in a single passage describing the heiress Geraldine in *An Indiscretion*. They therefore constitute a doublet which points to their common origin in *The Poor Man* so that we may say that the Lady of that novel already had the features of Fancy Day, or, given that Fancy's features are those of Tryphena, that in *The Poor Man and the Lady* its Lady was already a portrait of Tryphena Sparks. Geraldine shares these features and as a girl who 'looked more womanly than she really was' at the covert 1865 date of the narrative she is herself just as convincingly connected with Tryphena.

This is where Hardy's removal of 'some original verses' comes in. Prominent among the 'prosings' which eventually saw the light of day in *Desperate Remedies* are fragments of the 'She, to Him' sonnets which drew their inspiration from Tryphena's letters of the fall of 1865. If these were the poems which originally stood in the text of *The Poor Man* the heroine who is given Tryphena's looks must also - by way of the 'She, to Him' sonnets, which were ultimately derived from her letters - have been given her words as well.

With such affinities between the Lady of *The Poor Man* and Tryphena, we may guess that in some sense its Squire was a personation of Tryphena's father. Hardy certainly felt some animus towards the cabinet-making James Sparks. In the first edition of *Desperate Remedies* the 'extraordinary outline' of Miss Aldclyffe's dressing-table - 'something between a high altar and a cabinet piano' - is attributed to a local joiner named as 'Mr. James Sparkman'. Hardy later removed this lampoon on the man he had hoped to be his father-in-law, but it alerts us to the subterranean satire of the cabinet-making Parson Swancourt who has in his study just such another piece of furniture - a high table concocted from fragments of an old oak lych-gate.

This clue gives access to a consistent vein of satire. Swancourt is presented as a farmer who shouts up a field, as a man in shirtsleeves working on a roof, as a chair-maker who flings an ill-made chair across his workshop and as a man who curses and gets his daughter to write out his sermons for him. Under the mask of parson there seems to be a working man - and one of James Sparks's own trade. Not only does Parson Swancourt intercept his daughter's correspondence but, as a doublet in *An Indiscretion* shows, he also shares his town address in Chevron Square with Squire Allancourt from *The Poor Man*. Such details suggest the distinct possibility that the Squire of the lost novel was already a mask for the work-a-day James Sparks. This may explain Alexander Macmillan's incredulity at the characterisation of the Squire when he asks 'is it within the range of likelihood that any gentleman would pursue his wife at midnight and strike her?'[43]

But if it really is the Sparks family who secretly furnish the dramatis personae of *The Poor Man*, what induced Hardy to dress them up as gentry and raise them to that elevated status about which the satire of the novel hinged? An answer lies to hand in the précis that Celia Barclay gives of the reminiscences of Tryphena's nephew, Nathaniel Sparks Jr. From these reminiscences it appears that Jemima Hardy's elder sister Maria - Tryphena's mother - was translated from the poverty she had shared with her siblings to be sole heiress to the property of their well-off paternal grandfather, William Hand, and that Jemima herself regarded this preferment as an injustice she could never accept. In Jemima's eyes at least, Maria and her family had always been 'heiresses'. Given that Maria Sparks 'put a spoke' in Hardy's wheel when he tried to marry Tryphena and that the 1866 poem 'Postponement' presents a Hardy who found himself too poor to marry, we would seem to have all the ingredients here for Hardy's inducement to satirise the Sparks family as the intolerable grandees who put an end to the Poor Man's courtship of their daughter.

Such a concealment of country people under the mask of greatness is perhaps why, in the trailing detritus of the abandoned novel, we find the sly comment on the heiress Geraldine of *An Indiscretion* -

---

[43] The poem 'Her Father' is dated 'Weymouth 1869' in manuscript. Is this a more conciliatory view of James Sparks - but still retaining the implication of the father's opposition?

'the fine-lady portion of her existence, of which there was never much', or the baffling remark about the magnificent Miss Aldclyffe of *Desperate Remedies*, whose death is described in a verbatim doublet shared with Geraldine, that 'she was not so very unlike country girls of that type of beauty'.

XXIII - A DEPARTURE BY TRAIN

As Hardy completed *The Poor Man* Tryphena was facing her own difficulties. For 16 January 1868 the log of Puddletown School, where she had been engaged as Pupil Teacher since the start of 1867, has the entry - 'Reproved pupil teacher for neglect of duty - parents very angry in consequence - determine to withdraw her a month hence.' Tryphena's name does not appear in the logs of either the girls' or the boys' section of the school after 20 January, the H.M. Inspector's report for the following year shows she had been replaced by an M. George and in this same 1869 her own correspondence shows she was working somewhere well away from the Puddletown area.

What had Tryphena done? Mrs. Collins, the mistress, does not seem to have been quite sure. The entry I have quoted above was made retrospectively. This is clear from the fact that it was inserted into one of the blank lines in the log which are regularly left between the entries for one day and the next. On 20 January Tryphena was removed to the boys' section of the school and two days later Mrs. Collins 'explained fully' to her girls the seventh commandment - 'Thou shalt not commit adultery.' The exceptional significance of this *full* explanation of the single commandment may be gathered by contrasting it with Mrs. Collins routine entry of 16 May 1867 where a whole clutch of commandments are gathered together - 'Explained VI VII VIII commandments to first and second classes.' It is the seventh commandment which is painted up in vermilion letters as an accusation to Tess as she returns home from Trantridge as maiden no more.

Just here I am tempted to make a hypothetical reconstruction of events, for the derailment of Tryphena's career noticed in the Puddletown School log book seems to leave a mark in both Hardy's autobiography and in his fictions.

In *Life* Hardy opens a section with the heading '1868. January 16 and Onwards'. This is the sole heading in the autobiography to be attributed to a particular day of a particular month.[44] But the date indicates nothing more momentous than the start of fair-copying *The Poor Man*. Immediately Hardy goes on to note - 'In the February following a memorandum shows that he composed a lyric entitled 'A Departure by Train', which has disappeared.'

Long ago Southerington was suspicious of this juxtaposition of date and the redundant notice of a disappeared lyric. He asked whether it concealed some biographical event and of the train departure he asked - 'Who was going where? And why?' I think he was right

---

[44] Originally the entry was even more stark - it simply read '1868. January 16'. The typescript of *Life* shows that the words 'and Onwards' were added as an afterthought.

to be suspicious if only for the fact that in the fictions, in one guise or another, there seem to be no fewer than eleven paraphrases of a 'departure by train'. The recurrence is as obsessive as that of the sunset gnats or the 1865 calendar.

The first and fullest of these departures is the failed elopement of Stephen and Elfride in *A Pair of Blue Eyes*. This is the template of subsequent treatments of the theme which persist into Hardy's very latest fiction. Tryphena's memorial novel, *The Well-Beloved*, repeats variants of the railway elopement three times and *Jude* offers a final version.

There are numerous parallels which bind these scenes together. There are, for instance, the zinc chimney-pots shared by the railway episodes in *A Pair of Blue Eyes* and *The Well-Beloved*. Or, more significantly, the ubiquitous raindrops which 'beat like duck shot' on the window of Stephen and Elfride's carriage or, in *The Hand of Ethelberta*, whiz against it 'like a sower sowing his seed' which in *The Well-Beloved* becomes 'corn thrown in handfuls by some colossal sower' - a motif which ushers in numerous verbal parallelisms which betray the origin of these scenes in *The Poor Man*. Even the raindrops which tap 'like peas against the panes' alert us the fact that Hardy has used this and other details of the railway elopement scene to colour the tragic climax of *The Return of the Native*.[45]

---

[45] The opening scene in which Thomasin is returning from her failed marriage in the reddleman's cart looks like yet another variant of the motif. In *The Well-Beloved* the return train journey from London which Pierston and the second Avice make after their failed elopement is described as 'that wretched, never-to-be-forgotten day'. The emphatic nature of this

Such an obsession is not direct evidence of autobiography, but it may be significant that its latest incarnation in *Jude* draws perilously close to the story implied by the 1868 log of Puddletown School. Sue Bridehead is connected with Tryphena in her cousinship with the hero and in the details of her educational career. These connections no doubt point to Tryphena as the woman Hardy refers to in the Preface to the novel whose death in 1890 suggested 'some of the circumstances' of the story.[46] It is her railway outing with her cousin that leads to her withdrawal from the training college in just such an oblique and indecisive way as the log shows Tryphena to have departed from Puddletown School - not actively dismissed but with just the same unproven implication of moral opprobrium.

It seems to stretch credulity too far to suppose that it was by pure accident Hardy would give such a coherent narrative in *Jude the Obscure* and then re-assemble in his autobiography the key hints of a 'Departure by Train' and the date 16 January 1868 which inaugurated Tryphena's departure from Puddletown School. The unlikelihood - and the obsessive recurrence of this motif of 'a departure by train' - raises the distinct possibility that Hardy and Tryphena did indeed make some ill-considered rail journey - perhaps an attempted elopement - some time

---

expression is suggested by Hardy's retrospective construction of the note describing his last meeting with Horace Moule as 'A never-to-be-forgotten morning.'

[46] Millgate argues both for a different woman who had died in 1890 and then for the fact that 1890 is not meant anyway.

shortly before 16 January 1868 and that this was the background to Tryphena's altercation with Mrs. Collins.

XXIV - DESPAIR

If this reconstruction is correct the episode must have marked a significant moment in the disintegration of the cousins' affair - probably as a botched attempt to revive it. Stoically Hardy began fair-copying his novel on 16 January, but the final result does not find him in good spirits. On 9 June he completes the fair-copying. On 1 July he is entering into his journal 'Cures for despair' and when he reproduces the note in *Life* he says 'in all likelihood after a time of mental depression over his work and prospects.' In the context of the autobiography's general air of reticence the inclusion of this note and the commentary on it seem to admit a mood of exceptional distress. As late as the autumn a tone of disillusionment attaches itself to the novel. In September we find Hardy writing about *The Poor Man* to Macmillan, 'As the days go on, & you do not write, & my production begins to assume that small & unimportant shape everything one does assumes as the time & mood in which one did it recedes from the present I almost feel that I don't care what happens to the book, so long as something happens.'

In the autumn of 1868 Hardy rewrote some pages of *The Poor Man*[47], but the rest of this year was barren of

---

[47] Perhaps the ending, since both the poem 'A Poor Man and a Lady' and Hardy's account of the novel to Gosse suggest that at some time the book had an ending in which the heroine did not die, as she certainly had in the

any other production - apart from the sketches for 'Retty's Phases' and the nasty little stanza 'Gallant's Song'. There is therefore no evidence of the status of Hardy's engagement with Tryphena - unless it is to be found in the implications of 'Retty's Phases' - but the poems written in the next year make it pretty certain that it was in abeyance.

XXV - TRYPHENA AT A DISTANCE

It is not clear when Tryphena left the Puddletown area. It seems to have been some time between January 1868 and the November of that year when her mother died, for James Sparks's letters announcing his wife's death make it clear that Tryphena was not at her mother's bedside, though another of her sisters had been summoned from a distance. In 1869 she was certainly away from the area. In a letter of August written to her brother Nathaniel she describes herself as having only just returned home to Puddletown for a month's holiday.[48]

Such an absence is reflected in the poems Hardy wrote during his stay in Weymouth in 1869. There is

---

initial version seen by Macmillan. Hardy may have taken the opportunity of re-casting the ending to reflect the departure by train which could then have formed a textual basis for the numerous variants of this episode in subsequent novels.

[48] Tryphena may well have been in Blandford. Her late letter of 1888 refers to 'my old friends at Blandford' and the year 1868-9 seems to offer an inviting gap in her biography in which she could have made such friends. The MS. of 'My Cicely' shows a special expansion to include Blandford in the rider's itinerary - see Deacon and Coleman for a convincing argument that the poem concerns Tryphena's married life near Exeter.

'Singing Lovers' in which the poet contrasts the lovers of the title with his own love -

> But mine had gone away, -
> Whither, I shunned to say!

The distaste for her destination is more suggestive than informative. The girl is also called 'she of a bygone vow'. The word 'vow' surely implies an engagement and dovetails with the evidence I have already adduced for the engagement of the cousins. The girl's absence - *pace* Gittings - is also the theme of the poem 'At a Seaside Town in 1869'.

'At Waking' was written in 1869. Gittings's suggestion that the cancelled line 'Those words she had written awry' indicate that its vision was of a disillusioning letter is surely correct for the unfolding of such a hard letter seems to be caught in the compact ambiguity of the first stanza -

> I seemed to behold
> My love in bare
> Hard lines unfold.

The girl is described as a 'prize' which proves a blank. This is a characterisation which is indistinguishable from the 'lost prize' of 'Thoughts of Phena'. But such a refinement is scarcely necessary, for the assertion of the girl's absence in the 1869 poems and the evidence of Tryphena's own letter to her brother that she was indeed absent from the area at this time make it highly likely that it was she who was the writer of the disillusioning letter that lies behind the poem.[49]

Despite such moments of bitterness, with his rowing and swimming in Weymouth Bay and his dalliance in a quadrille class, Hardy paints a picture of himself in the summer of 1869 as a man who had forgotten what it was to be intense. All this was soon to change.

XXVI - THE COMPOSITION OF DESPERATE REMEDIES

Hardy began *Desperate Remedies* in the autumn of 1869. The book was the first fruit of his decision to abandon *The Poor Man*. He gives us a sort of explanation of his decision to suppress *The Poor Man* in an account of his early authorship concealed under the literary career of Ethelberta. She tells us that when she ceased to write verse she turned to a prose story. This transition recalls the abandonment of verse with the poems of 1865-7 in favour of *The Poor Man* and the description of the prose story - 'It was written in the first person and its style was modelled after De Foe's' - clearly indicates *The Poor Man*. But on the eve of publication she decides to retain the manuscript of this

---

[49]Millgate notes the characterisation of Tryphena as 'prize' in 'Thoughts of Phena' but in 'At Waking' where the woman is also described as 'prize' he denies any connection with Tryphena on the basis that 'the word is common enough in Hardy's work'. But this would only be an argument if Millgate could show that such other occurrences are not also references to Tryphena - the context of 'At Waking' now makes it clear that this 'prize' at any rate almost certainly does refer to Tryphena and the same can be said of the emphatic use of the word in *A Pair of Blue Eyes*.

prose tale - 'convinced that I should do better by telling the story.' Her telling of tales becomes her livelihood.

Hardy is revealing a good deal about the start of his prose career here. *The Poor Man* had indeed come to the verge of publication. Tinsley had offered terms for it, but Hardy withdrew the book in September 1869 in order to begin 'telling the story'. This kind of telling explains Hardy's persistent recourse to *The Poor Man* even into his latest prose fiction. *The Well-Beloved* betrays a whole web of verbal and motivic details shared with much earlier novels like *The Hand of Ethelberta*. The persistent outcropping of doublets throughout the novels suggests that the theory set afoot by Weber of Hardy's economic parcelling out of the text of *The Poor Man* among his early novels must be substantially erroneous. There is only evidence for two limited instances of such a cannibalisation. Against this the evidence of the doublets shows that far from expending the text in economic fashion Hardy reworked some of its key moments over and over again, so thoroughly transforming them that on some occasions only a close textual analysis reveals their common origin. This is clearly the case with the sunset gnats and very probably with the departure by train. This continuity shows that in some sense the Wessex Novels are still *telling* the story of *The Poor Man* - a circumstance vouched for both by the outcropping of the doublets and by the persistent calendar for 1865 which appears to have underlain the lost work.

These later evolutions no doubt explain why *The Poor Man* had to be destroyed. Hardy rather mysteriously claimed he had got rid of the manuscript when he was moving. Some pages of it survived until shortly before his death, but he burned them. *The Poor Man* would have revealed the original contexts of those passages Hardy reworked over and over again - it would have given an insight into the telling of its story in the Wessex Novels that would demand explanation. One can only imagine what it cost Hardy to destroy this work which as a septuagenarian he was to call 'the most original thing (for its date) that I ever wrote.'

Meredith, in his interview of March 1869, seems to have convinced Hardy that *The Poor Man* was too 'pronounced a thing', that he should not nail his colours to the mast 'if he wished to do anything practical in literature'. The modification of the first person of *The Poor Man* into the third person narrative of *Desperate Remedies* and the subsequent Wessex Novels was evidence of a new attempt to do something practical.[50]

But a very impractical motive for this practicality is written into the second part of *An Indiscretion*. Here once more is an account of Hardy's early authorship. *The Poor Man* is passed over as 'a book which nobody ever heard of' and Mayne's next book is, as I have already shown, meticulously defined as *Desperate Remedies* by its two word title, its anonymous publication and its laudatory reviews in three weighty

---

[50] A view Hardy had already reached himself before Meredith's intervention. In his September 1868 letter to Macmillan the sentence 'The earlier fancy, that *Hamlet* without Hamlet would never do turns to a belief that it would be better than closing the house.' seems to anticipate the abandonment of the first person narrative of *The Poor Man* for the third person narrative characteristic of the Wessex Novels.

literary periodicals. These details do not merely secure the date-peg which sets up the chronology of the novella. *Desperate Remedies* itself is an important character of the drama, for this book of Mayne's is designed to win back the hand of the heiress Geraldine from whom he has been parted. The story is emphatic on this point. Mayne's shock is overwhelming when Geraldine does not respond to his literary success - 'is this all I get after this lapse of time and heat of labour?' he cries with raw emotion.

This fictional moment has every appearance of being a real reflection of Hardy's motives in the summer of 1870.[51] In *Life* he calls *Desperate Remedies* 'a sort of thing he had never contemplated writing, till, finding himself in a corner, it seemed necessary to attract public attention at all hazards.' The autobiography does not explain to us what sort of a 'corner' this was, but the urgency seems real enough. Hardy recalls ignoring Crickmay's repeated summons to go down to St. Juliot until he had posted off the MS. of the novel to Macmillan. Then, quite unaccountably, the urgency evaporates. Hardy describes his mood when he had gone up to London in May - 'He seems to have passed the days in Town desultorily and dreamily...and it is not clear what he was waiting for there.' The summer passes and 'Nothing seems to have

---

[51] In strict consistency the allusion to the publication of *Desperate Remedies* (March 1871) should place this phase of the narrative in 1871. But if we are to read this part of *An Indiscretion* as autobiography, Hardy may have allowed himself the license of telescoping events because *Desperate Remedies* was already in Tinsley's hands in the spring of 1870 and could therefore play the part of the inducement to marriage attributed to it in *An Indiscretion*.

been done about the novel.' It is the story told in *An Indiscretion* which seems to explain this volte face.

Mayne's *femme inspiratrice*, Geraldine, is linked with Tryphena both as a girl who is 'such a child' at a date of 1865 and at this same date one whose fineness of figure makes her look 'more womanly than she really was'. There may also be a parallel between Hardy's motives for writing *Desperate Remedies* and Mayne's motive for writing a book which so explicitly imitates the publishing details of *Desperate Remedies*. Tryphena entered college in London in January 1870. It must have been now that in the phrase of Mrs. Bromell, Tryphena's daughter, Hardy was 'tacking after' her mother at college. Tryphena was now clear of the immediate influence of her family. But Hardy still had to contend with her own feelings about their union. His last meeting with his cousin in July 1870 was to prove disastrous. The hero of 'The Revisitation' recalls the heroine's 'too proud temper ruling that had parted us before'. But this was a denouement Hardy could have anticipated. The 1869 poem 'At Waking' starkly lays out the psychological conditions under which he would have every reason to vacillate. The poem acknowledges the crushing effect of a discouraging letter. The poet can only oppose this finality by a desperate act of will - 'Off: it is not true;/For it cannot be....' But what he cannot shake off is the suspicion that 'the prize I drew/Is a blank to me!' When Hardy speaks of passing his time 'desultorily and dreamily' in the capital he may well have feared such a negative result and delayed the moment of truth as long as he could. Such indecision explains Mayne's conduct - 'whether he should stand forth visibly before her or keep in the background seemed a question of life or death.' In the event it is weeks before he stands forth and he is then rejected.

It is hard to resist the conclusion that Mayne's hesitation in facing Geraldine has some connection with Hardy's failure to do anything about the novel. Did Hardy need his cousin's approval before committing his slender worldly resources to the publication of *Desperate Remedies*? *An Indiscretion* implies that Hardy had intended the book as a demonstration of his ability to make an income and thereby a convincing proposition as a husband. Such a motive would throw a brilliant retrospective light on the precise timing of the 'Departure by Train'. That escapade - if I am right in my tentative reconstruction of it - had coincided with the completion of *The Poor Man*. So there may be a pattern here. With *The Poor Man* his completion of a first attempt at the novel may have given Hardy the confidence to tempt Tryphena into the rail journey which indirectly led to her withdrawal from Puddletown School - just as the completion of *Desperate Remedies* emboldened him to make contact with Tryphena once again when she was at college in London.

If this parallel holds, the beginning of Hardy's prose authorship with both *The Poor Man* and *Desperate Remedies* would seem to have had the perfectly consistent motive of representing himself as a husband to Tryphena. He does not seem to have remembered that antipathy to literary fame expressed in the sonnet 'Her Reproach', though the sonnet has every appearance of being a translation of Tryphena's aversion to his ambition from one of her own letters. By the time he came to write *An Indiscretion* in the wake of Tryphena's marriage to Charles Gale it was no doubt a wiser and a sadder Hardy who transferred the mocking image of 'Fame's far summits' from 'Her Reproach' to the account of Mayne's authorship.

XXVII - CORNISH RESERVATIONS

On 7 March 1870 Hardy went to Cornwall to make preliminary plans for the restoration of the church at St. Juliot. There he met Emma Gifford, who at once noticed the blue paper manuscript of a poem sticking out of his pocket. The Cornish romance is such an oasis in the general desert of what has certainly been known about Hardy's emotional life that a biographer may rather lose his head. Enthusiasm obscures what must have been foremost in Hardy's mind at this particular juncture. He had just packed off the manuscript of *Desperate Remedies*. The novel had a calendar centred on 1865, it contained a portrait of the teenage Tryphena and even seems to have been an instrument Hardy hoped would sway his cousin. He had yet to confront Tryphena face to face. He would do so in the July - with fatal consequences. The logic of this reconstruction is that - anticipating such an explanation with his cousin - he cannot have helped but carry her image with him into Cornwall. There are hints that this was the case. When he visits Beeny Cliff for the first time with Emma on 10 March a fragment of his journal note gives "The tender grace of a day', etc.' Nobody has commented on the precise notation.

The little 'etc.' draws attention to the words from Tennyson's 'Break, break, break' which Hardy did not choose to quote -

> But the tender grace of a day that is dead
> Will never come back to me.

Beeny only serves to remind Hardy of a day that is dead. This may have been the August day of 1865 when he visited Portland with Tryphena - at least, Tennyson's poem is more suggestive of Portland than of Beeny; it has ships that 'go on/To their haven under the hill' and a lad who 'sings in his boat on the bay' like the Weymouth Bay of the 1869 poem 'Singing Lovers'.

This may be a first hint that recollections that did not belong to the Cornish scene still obtrude themselves upon it. By 1873 such transplanted recollections had taken on large literary dimensions. As work on *A Pair of Blue Eyes* progressed the figure of Tryphena was to become thoroughly domesticated in this new landscape. Hardy gave the novel a calendar for 1865 and he remembered this when he told Hermann Lea that Elfride had some similarities with an Emma 'as she showed herself in youth', or, as *Life* puts it, with an Emma 'in quite young womanhood, a few years before Hardy met her'. Given the novel's 1865 calendar how circumstantial this 'few years' is! The climax of the narrative arrives in chapter twenty-one where Knight's precarious hold on the brow of the cliff and the persistent sexual imagery evoke the realities of summer 1865 with the Matterhorn disaster and Hardy's sexual encounter with a young cousin who seems to govern the characterisation of Elfride as 'infantine' girl/woman and to provide her with the autumn correspondence which succeeded the first flush of her affair. Such details are part of the secret subtext of the narrative. It is extraordinary that they should have been hidden under the outward semblance of the young lady from St. Juliot rectory. Hardy finds an epigraph for the climactic chapter on the brow of the cliff from the now familiar Tennyson lyric 'Break, break, break' with the line 'On thy cold gray stones, O sea!' He has not added a little 'etc.' but he might well have done, for the lines continue 'And I would that my tongue could utter/The thoughts that arise in me.'

Hardy may have prepared himself for the trauma of his first stay at the rectory by making his blue poetic manuscript catch the eye. Emma was herself an author. By the autumn of 1870 she was fair-copying chapters of *Desperate Remedies*. In the following year, when Hardy mooted abandoning novel-writing, she 'wrote back instantly her desire that he should adhere to authorship.' Scribe and comforter she may have been, but that did not admit her to the inner world of *A Pair of Blue Eyes*. Years later her exclusion is rather heartlessly announced in the 1895 Preface to the novel when Hardy evokes the Cornish coast.

> The place is pre-eminently (for one person at least) the region of dream and mystery. The ghostly birds, the pall-like sea, the frothy wind, the eternal soliloquy of the waters, the bloom of dark purple cast that seems to exhale from the shoreward precipices, in themselves lend to the scene an atmosphere like the twilight of a night vision.

The parenthesis 'for one person at least' is pointed and public - Hardy would only read Emma's parallel evocation of the Cornish coast in her *Recollections* after she was dead. In 1895 he sees her as incapable of entering into the 'dark purple' symbolism with which he invests it. It is not the bright purple of *porphureos*, but Tryphena's symbolic colour - the 'dark purple' of *phoenix* for Phena which Hardy drew from his Greek lexicon. It was also a Victorian colour of mourning and this alerts us to the emphatically funereal re-colouring of the coastal scene with its ghostly birds and pall-like sea.[52] The precise date of the Preface is March 1895 - a March which brought the fifth anniversary of Tryphena's death. March was also the month in which Hardy first visited Beeny in 1870, his mood a quarter of a century later still chimed with that first impression which had reminded him of 'a day that is dead'.

There is a hint here of the archeological strata that lie hidden under the surface of the Cornish Romance. Just as Hardy has shifted the date of his severe illness to cover the year 1865, so his bleak parting from Tryphena is hidden by the prompt start of his romance at St. Juliot. There can be little doubt that Hardy indulged an element of retrospective construction in suggesting the sudden onset of his official romance. For instance, the date of composition of 'The Sun on the Bookcase' in which Hardy at Bockhampton muses on the distant

---

[52] q.v. Tess's appearance at the Sandbourne lodging house 'in half-mourning tints' - custom dictated that purple succeeded the black of 'deep mourning'. See Appendix for the symbolism of *phoenix* and it's reference to the poem 'Alike and Unlike' for a precisely analogous use of Tryphena's symbolic purple to exclude Emma.

Emma is given as 1872 in manuscript and only altered to 1870 for subsequent publication. With this new date it bolsters assertions of an instant romance proposed by the poem 'When I set out for Lyonnesse'.[53]

Hardy certainly proved sensitive about the presentation of his arrival in Cornwall. In his transcription of Emma's *Some Recollections* there is the sentence 'So I met my husband, or rather he met me.' Hardy did not like the tone of the last five words. In his transcription they are inked through though still legible. But in Emma's manuscript the offending words are inked over so as to be totally blotted out. Clearly Hardy could read them when he made his transcription. It must be Hardy who has subsequently inked them over in the manuscript. It seems to have been the same sensitivity which led him to amend the sense of another sentence in Emma's manuscript that now begins, 'At first, though I was interested in him, the church-matters were paramount.' It seems unintelligible that on Emma's part this sentence should

---

[53] The calendar and hidden references of *A Pair of Blue Eyes* show that Hardy had imported Tryphena into the Cornish scene by 1873. She may already have been there in March 1870 when Beeny had reminded Hardy of a 'day that is dead'. Is the image of Tryphena in Hardy's mind the real and obvious explanation of the Interloper in the poem of that name? Is the 'cowled Apparition' of 'At the Piano' a kindred interloper, as Purdy suggests? Curiously the 'figure' of the pencil sketch which Hardy made in the rain on Beeny Cliff on 22 August 1870 is also 'cowled'. It is only in the ink transcription of this sketch that Hardy has made the 'figure' sit up - the original pencil sketch shows it awkwardly slumped against the right-hand margin. But this outline is surely the outline of the cliff itself - one drawn too far right for Hardy's composition so that he redrew the cliff at the centre of the sketch, returning to the outline he had started with and fancifully converting it into a 'figure' by scribbling in the adumbration of a hand and turning the precise outline of the cliff's brow into a hood or cowl.

have demanded the forest of scrubbings out, additions and relocations the manuscript shows, rather than simply starting again. From the spacing and what remains of the original words, the sentence seems simply to have read, 'At first I was not greatly interested in him for the church matters were paramount.' This was evidently a statement Hardy disliked even more than 'So I met my husband, or rather he met me.'

On his own behalf Hardy can admit that 'He was soon, if not immediately, struck by the nature and appearance of the lady who received him.' But his biographers are more impatient. Millgate dogmatically assigns the kiss of the poem 'At the Word 'Farewell'' to Hardy's first visit to St. Juliot in March 1870, though Hardy himself distinctly says the poem 'seems to refer to this or the following visit'. It is a lead that Tomalin follows. For us Hardy's refusal to decide between his first visit in March or his second visit in August as the date of the kiss might now be seen as a miserable equivocation. Between this March and this August falls the blow of his last interview with Tryphena in the July.

I do not know that we are now in a position to understand Hardy. Certainly the subtext of his hopes of Tryphena - hopes which must still have been alive on his earliest visit to Cornwall - must qualify our view of the start of his and Emma's romance. The subtext of *A Pair of Blue Eyes* suggests there was an element of persistent duplicity in Hardy's courtship. Indeed, it begs the question of exactly what sort of courtship this was.

Millgate assures us that after his second visit of August 1870 Hardy 'considered himself betrothed'. Hardy himself is a little more cautious. Writing of January 1871 he speaks of himself as 'virtually if not distinctly engaged to be married' and if Millgate is right in thinking Emma and the Holders were trying to trap Hardy into marriage this is all the more weighty a qualification. The real meaning of this admission is surely exposed in the snippets from two of Emma's letters which Hardy preserved in a notebook. In the first letter, of October 1870, Emma is now more than interested in Hardy. This is how he enters the two-part excerpt from the first of these letters -

> "This dream of my life - no, not dream, for what is actually going on around me seems a dream rather...' And: 'I take him - the reserved man - as I do the Bible: find out what I can, compare one text with another, and believe the rest in a simple lump of faith."

'This dream of my life' seems to betray the fact that these extracts are taken from a love letter. After the rebuff of July 1870 Hardy was on the rebound - at least, he had been sufficiently bold or vulnerable to engage Emma's feelings. In this autumn Emma was fair-copying the manuscript of *Desperate Remedies* for him. The other letter was written in July 1874, two months before their marriage, while Hardy was at work on *Far from the Madding Crowd* and this is how he records the two excerpts from this later letter -

> 'My work, unlike your work of writing, does not occupy my true mind much...' 'Your novel seems

sometimes like a child, all your own and none of me.'

It is extraordinary how Hardy preserves from both these letters two excerpts which might almost be called antithetical. The first snippet of each pair makes clear that Emma's inner mind is with Hardy - the second her sense that Hardy's inner mind is not with her. These were the only snippets from Emma's letters Hardy was to preserve and their careful selection tacitly bespeaks his guilt at a withdrawal of which Emma seems to have been vaguely aware both early in her romance and shortly before marriage.

By the time *Far From the Madding Crowd* had begun to appear in serial form Millgate makes the pertinent suggestion 'that as his marriage became more feasible in economic terms Hardy became increasingly uncertain as to its wisdom.' Millgate instances his attractions to other women of literary or artistic connections. But for Emma the real difficulty of her romance was that Hardy was already wedded to authorship - that authorship already usurped one of the prime functions of marriage in that his novel seemed 'sometimes like a child.' The ruthlessness of authorship is evident in the secret bravado of flattering Emma by giving Elfride the public appearance of Miss Gifford, while all along his heroine remained the infantine girl of 1865. In the event marriage was to end what Millgate calls in some respects the 'most generously creative period' of Hardy's career. From the fertility of *Far From the Madding Crowd* Hardy descends into the sterility of *Ethelberta* whose charms, such as they are, are a very muted repetition of earlier work.

XXVIII - STANDING BY THE MANTELPIECE

July 1870 was the last time Hardy and Tryphena were to see each other. 'The Revisitation' suggests the tone of their parting - 'In a joyless hour of discord' with the young woman's 'too proud temper ruling.' It was to be another eighteen months before Tryphena moved to Plymouth and took up her post as headmistress. She met Charles Gale, they became friendly and he pressed her to return Hardy's ring. I am tempted to date the return of the ring to the summer of 1873. It may well have been the last direct contact between the cousins.

Heavy weather has been made of the interpretation of 'Standing by the Mantelpiece' - a record of Hardy's last evening with his friend Horace Moule in the June of 1873. Millgate gets as far as admitting the obvious - that it is Hardy himself who is being addressed by Moule in the poem - only to suggest that Hardy has been 'surprised' by a homosexual approach from Moule. The speaker says -

> Since you agreed, unurged and full-advised,
> And let warmth grow without discouragement,
> Why do you bear you now as if surprised,
> When what has come was clearly consequent?

Millgate's interpretation may appear daring, but it overlooks the biographical context of the poem. Its scene is set on the evening of 20 June 1873, the last evening on which Hardy was to see Moule. The next day Hardy travelled on to Bath where Emma Gifford was staying. *Life* gives details of his ten day visit, seeing the sights with an Emma who was sometimes chaperoned by her friend Miss d'Arville and sometimes alone with him. Hardy's poem 'Midnight on Beechen, 187-' - one of almost embarrassing feebleness - betrays the theme of his contemplation on this hill overlooking Bath.

> The city sleeps below. I sigh,
> For there dwells one, all testify,
> To match the maddest dream's desire:
> What swain with her would not aspire
> To walk the world, yea, sit but nigh
> On Beechen Cliff!

'Walk the world' surely implies that this is the meditation of a man trying to make up his mind to marriage.

In this context Moule's words in 'Standing by the Mantelpiece' can really only bear one interpretation - it is between himself and Emma Gifford that Hardy has let warmth grow to the point where he has no decent alternative but to propose. It was now, I suppose, that his virtual engagement became distinct.[54]

By the strangest coincidence a poem called 'The Future' was just about to be penned by Charles Gale for Tryphena. It begins 'All before us lies the way/Give the past unto the wind.' But there is rather a troubling amount about the past, for the proper 'way' can only be got into when 'all error is worked out' and when 'the

---

[54] See Henry Reed's notes (quoted by Rabiger in *Hardy Review*, autumn 2011, p.128.) of a conversation with Florence Hardy in 1936 in which the foregoing interpretation of 'Standing by the Mantelpiece' is unequivocally endorsed.

sensuous is laid low' and when 'the soul to sin hath died'. With these provisos Gale now looks forward to Eden days in a 'spirit land' of 'immortal unity'. I take it that this is the offering of a newly engaged and earnest Victorian young man who is aware that his bride to be has a past. Hardy would have made a better job of the verse, but the lines suggest there must have been a painful explanation for Tryphena of the kind Tess makes on her wedding night and that Gale's response had a generosity beyond Angel Clare's scope. The poem is dated July 1873.

There may, of course, be nothing very extraordinary in this dating. It may be that Hardy's musings on Beechen Cliff and Gale's romantic hymnody have a direct connection - that both the cousins could contemplate marriage to their prospective partners because one had decided to formally release the other. So this was perhaps the date at which Tryphena returned Hardy's ring.

Of course, authorship plays its part in the timing. *A Pair of Blue Eyes* had been published just three weeks before Hardy saw Moule for the last time in Cambridge. Hardy and Emma caught the first of the reviews of the book in their walks about Bath. So Hardy was now entitled to become engaged - or the success of the book meant he had lost his last defence *against* becoming engaged. Perhaps he had been rash to let the blue paper of a poem in manuscript stick out of his pocket on that first meeting with Emma on the evening of 7 March 1870.

This would not be the first time we could detect the influence of authorship on the question of marriage. It is there in Hardy's puzzling neglect of the manuscript of *Desperate Remedies* while he was nerving himself to confront Tryphena in the summer of 1870, or again, as I have suggested, in the coincidence of the completion of *The Poor Man* with a departure by train. *Far From the Madding Crowd* was finished in July 1874. Hardy and Emma were married in the September.

XXIX - SOME TECHNICAL MATTERS

Family communication no doubt kept Hardy abreast of the substantial changes in Tryphena's life - her marriage, her children, her illness and death. From time to time there seems to be evidence of such awareness. But after July 1870 Tryphena must largely have become a figure of musing and recollection for Hardy. The story of his affair with his cousin has its importance in his biography. The shadow Tryphena casts onto even Hardy's latest fiction suggests that Lois Deacon was not far wrong in her estimate of the affair as 'a tragic and enduring love-story'. But the story itself proves an illumination of quite technical matters. It takes us inside Hardy's workshop so that we can see in some cases how he laid out the large-scale architecture of his books. I have made this clear enough in the case of *The Well-Beloved*, but the 1865 calendars also give a privileged insight into the construction of other stories.

After the picaresque looseness of *The Poor Man* Meredith had encouraged Hardy to apply 'more plot' and in *Desperate Remedies* he did so with a vengeance.[55] The plot of *The Poor Man*, narrated as it was in the first person by the Poor Man, must have had a certain linear quality. In *Desperate Remedies* the narration withdraws into the third person and the single hero is split into two. One only has to look at the introductory portraits of the two heroes - Springrove and Manston - to see how literally Hardy has followed out his conception. They are two clones of a hidden original. It seems likely that Hardy was already referring to this transformation of *The Poor Man* when in 1868 he wrote to Macmillan of recasting the book as '*Hamlet* without Hamlet'.

Once Hardy has split his original hero into two he has to reduplicate the calendar in which their stories are told. The 1865 which appears to have underlain the 'simple' plot of *The Poor Man* is split into an 1864 of Springrove's romance with Cytherea and an 1865 of her romance with Manston. But the fact that 1865 is the 'real' year of Hardy's own romance persists in the most extraordinary way, for the 1864 span of the narrative is introduced by a coherent sequence of references to events of 1865. There is Ambrose Graye's fall from the church spire, modeled on the Matterhorn disaster of July 1865. There is the disintegration of his architectural practice - a reference to Hardy's own inability to hold down his job in the summer of 1865 - and the vision of his son Owen traveling down to Dorset through a parched summer landscape which imitates the exceptional meteorological conditions of

---

[55]Even with a sense of cynicism as the sarcastic explanation of passing over the 'Aldclyffe state dinner' suggests - a sarcasm he suppressed after the first edition.

the real 1865. This cluster of events projecting Hardy's own return to Dorset in this summer of exceptional heat could be taken as Hardy's note to himself that this introduction to the explicit 1864 of the novel's calendar redefines it as an alternative version of 1865.

Such a scheme was further sophisticated in *A Pair of Blue Eyes*. Here once more there is an explicit 1864 of Stephen's romance followed by the 1865 of Knight's romance. But Hardy has gone to much greater lengths to make one year a shadowy parallel of the other, even to the extent of confusing himself when Elfride's exploit on the church tower is compared with a giddy feat of the year before - of which the narrative of the earlier year itself knows nothing at all. But 1865 is still the 'real' year that is unfolded in the presentation of two successive years. Hardy has symmetrically disposed the ages of his two heroes - twenty and thirty - around his own age in 1865. This was the year he became a young man and the index of this 'development in virility' is the appearance of masculine moustache and beard. In the novel's 1864 Stephen is pointedly hairless. In its 1865 Knight is pointedly hirsute. When Stephen returns in the explicit 1865 of the novel's calendar he now has his moustache.[56]

Tess makes this interpretation of Hardy's strategy quite certain. Once again Tess's story is presented as the succession of contrasted lovers, but the changes

---

[56] This interpretation of the calendar of *A Pair of Blue Eyes* also argues that the 'real' date of the lovers' correspondence imitated from *The Poor Man* is autumn 1865. This is an argument which also brings Cytherea's correspondence with Springrove into the fold of these references to Tryphena's letters of the fall of 1865.

Hardy made in his manuscript show how carefully he has adjusted the ages of his heroes - twenty four and twenty six - to be once more symmetrically disposed around his own age in 1865 and, in co-ordination with these changes, how careful are the manuscript alterations in the detail of Alec and Angel's state of beard to suit their roles as 'young men' in the specific sense the story of Hardy's relations with his cousin implies. The transition between the 'fuzz' with which Alec first appears and the 'shapely moustache and beard' of Angel pinpoints the arrival of young manhood - the change Hardy himself dates to the age of 'five-and-twenty'. This is why the manuscript changes which finalise the exact ages of Alec and Angel coincide with those which which distinguish the two heroes' state of beard - together the ages and the beards make up an integral portrait of the Hardy who became a young man in 1865. The hovering duplication of the years in which Tess is seduced and in which she capitulates to Clare is sedulously notated in introducing the sunset gnats into both the eve of Tess's seduction by Alec and into the eve of her capitulation to Clare. In the latter phase of the story the verbal traces of *The Poor Man* are all too evident in the gnats, the description of the meads and the limp rhubarb leaves like half-closed umbrellas which, in *The Return of the Native* and in *Desperate Remedies*, had given a picture of the real weather of 1865.

The cloning of his heroes probably explains a certain depletion of vitality in them - Hardy is spreading one person rather thinly. There is evidence that he clung to a single portrait - or self-portrait - as tenaciously as he clung to the year 1865. In their introductory portraits the two 1865 heroes of *Desperate Remedies*, Springrove and Manston, show themselves as clones of a single original. Notoriously Clym Yeobright has 'the typical countenance of the future'. But Somerset in *A Laodicean* also has the beauty 'of the future human type' - a motif implicit in Springrove's thought-weary look 'seeming to state, 'I have already thought out the issues of such conditions as these we are experiencing.'' Once the superficial details are stripped away the introductory portrait of Somerset's rival, De Stancy, appears to be modeled on precisely the same formula as that of Springrove in *Desperate Remedies*.

Reduplication is not the only way to elaborate an 1865. In *The Return of the Native* Hardy adapts his discovery of the dual hero by folding their stories back into a single 1865 - the calendar actually runs from autumn 1864 to autumn 1865 - so that Clym inherits the sunset gnats of the summer romance and Wildeve the transmogrified details of the 'Departure by Train'.[57] Symbolically, at the catastrophe of the plot, the upper and lower man are dragged from the water locked in a tight embrace.

The Well-Beloved may represent Hardy's ultimate ingenuity in constructing an elaborate architecture out of his reminiscences of Tryphena, but *Jude the Obscure*

---

[57] Compare the rain-drops 'like peas against the panes' and the drying of the bank-notes before the fire with the rain 'like the pellets of a pop-gun' and the drying of clothes in Pierston and Marcia's elopement or the same circle of images in the wake of Jude and Sue's train excursion - passages which first break surface in *A Pair of Blue Eyes*.

betrays at least touches of such autobiographical structuring. Hardy was in two minds about drawing attention to this structure, priding himself that the plot was 'almost geometrically constructed', but claiming 'the rectangular lines of the story were not premeditated.' The characterisation was certainly schematic. Hardy wrote in 1889 in the midst of work on *Tess* - and when his heroine was still called Sue - that the most suitable title for the story would be 'The Body and Soul of Sue'. In *Jude* he has pursued this dichotomy by making Arabella a 'substantial female animal' and pushing Sue Bridehead as far as he can in the direction of a neurotic soulfulness.[58]

Their undivided original, Tess, had been identified with Tryphena by the adaptation of the journal note of 15 March 1890. In *Jude* the divided aspects implicit in Tess Durbeyfield still retain traces of Tryphena - most obviously in the case of Sue Bridehead. Sue is both cousin and school-mistress and her expectation that she will 'pass pretty high' and get 'a big school' is a thumbnail sketch of Tryphena's career at Stockwell College and in Plymouth.[59] In her story there seem also

---

[58] The process of breaking the heroine into antithetical personae is under way in 'On the Western Circuit' and *The Well-Beloved*. The short story breaks her unity into the 'unlettered peasant' who is Anna and her educated mistress. In the novel Avice I is 'a refined and well-informed woman' in contrast with Avice II who is 'almost illiterate' - though both are surrogates for Tryphena, as the dual heroines of the short story also appear to be.

[59] The motif of cousinship is shared by all three of these 'last' novels. In *Jude* it is explicit. In *The Well-Beloved* Pierston and Avice's families are interrelated. In *Tess* Joan Durbeyfield calls Alex her daughter's cousin and in an insertion into the manuscript we find Alex's words and the comment - '"Cousin" Tess ["Cousin" had a faint ring of mockery].' I give Hardy's punctuation.

to be references to Tryphena's departure from Puddletown School in 1868 and to her presence in London in 1870. But Arabella equally retains hints of Tryphena. The stream by which she first appears may adumbrate the 'sparkling river' in front of the Sparks' house in Puddletown and her coiled-up hair seems to have been borrowed from the heavy coil of hair we see in photographs of Tryphena. According to Tryphena's daughter her mother had 'dark chestnut hair, heaps of it.' When Angel sees Tess again 'her well-remembered cable of dark-brown hair was partially coiled up in a mass at the back of her head'. We read of the hair which Arabella wore 'twisted in an enormous knob at the back of her head'. We are told that at the Training School Sue's 'hair, which formerly she had worn according to the custom of the day, was now twisted up tightly.' Tryphena's daughter, Mrs. Bromell, was told that when her mother went to college 'she put her hair up in a coronet'. Arabella and Sue - as the schematic clue of 'The Body and Soul of Sue' suggested - are merely another in the long line of Hardy's bifurcations. As always Hardy seems to have inserted into the novel a private memorandum of their hidden unity. At their first meeting he says of Jude and Arabella, 'They walked in parallel lines.' At Jude and Sue's first meeting once again 'They walked on in parallel lines.' There is certainly something geometrical going on here.

Of course, this little construction - for the reader keen enough to notice it - may have an aesthetic effect and it is one which can be entrusted to a reader. I am interested in tracing such details in another direction. I suggested that Hardy himself associated the stream by which Arabella appears with the 'sparkling river' in front of the Sparks' house in Puddletown. This looks pretty certain from the ancestry of the motif in 'Destiny and a Blue Cloak'. There the stream separates the mill from the high road in honour of Tryphena's home in Mill Street - a reference which dovetails with the battery of other allusions to the Sparks' household in the short story. The stream is crossed by 'a little wood bridge' which is the scene of Oswald and Agatha's romantic *tête-à-tête* on the eve of their separation. Jude's first *tête-à-tête* with Arabella is conducted on 'the small plank bridge' which crosses Arabella's stream. The small wooden bridge to the Sparks' front door must have become a place of fear and exaltation for Hardy - the spot at which he entered the magic circle of the Sparks family and the spot at which Tryphena might be detached from that circle.

This ramification may be a little speculative - but my attempt is to show what Hardy's writing meant to him, as much as what it may mean to us. Of course, the two areas overlap in a rather hazy way. This might be the point to define the 'autobiographical' a little more closely. But this too is an idea that cannot be very clearly defined. In the novels and poems I have isolated various elements drawn from Hardy's life. They are sufficiently repetitive, indeed obsessive, for us to say such a reliance on his own story is especially important for Hardy's art. But does Hardy use the details of his experience in order to write, or does he write in order to enshrine these experiences? Both may be simultaneously true. Of course, it is equally true that strictly speaking I have not *isolated* such elements - they are always shading off into pure fiction. Or, should I say, a rather impure fiction - just to the extent that the calendars and the biographical circumstances Hardy puts into his novels have from their very obsessive repetition a slightly detachable quality.[60]

Overwhelmingly these repeated elements have to do with a story that begins in 1865 and for all intents and purposes is done with by 1870. The reminiscence of these few years is Hardy's literary capital. In the Wessex Novels he does better by 'telling the story' rather than squandering it in the generous, spendthrift pages of *The Poor Man*. If Hardy is to redeploy these elements so that they retain their emotional charge for him without betraying their presence by too literal a repetition he must become a master of disguise. I have shown the arcane means by which he conceals the 1865 calendar by ever more subtle disguises. *In A Pair of Blue Eyes* the 'double 1865' plot is at its most schematic. *Desperate Remedies* and *Tess* also have a 'double 1865' plot, but in these novels it is more heavily disguised. The bifurcation of biographical originals - if we are to take Arabella and Sue as in some sense aspects of Tryphena Sparks, or Angel and Alec as versions of Hardy himself as a young man - might also be called a kind of disguise. Or it is an elaboration or extension - even an eking out - of the materials which belonged to

---

[60] The most curious indication of the extra-fictional nature of the fictions is Hardy's punctuation of the last line of *The Pursuit of the Well-Beloved* - "'O - no, no! I - I - it is too, too droll - this ending to my would-be romantic history!" Ho-ho-ho!' As Millgate notes the 'Ho-ho-ho!' is 'outside quotation marks and hence presumably authorial.' However opaque, this authorial intervention subverts the fictionality of everything that has gone before - pointing, in my analysis, to the biographical meaning of the work.

the life Hardy lived between 1865 and 1870. But behind such technical explanations there lies a more fundamental uncertainty. Ultimately it is the vexed question of whether Geraldine, or Lucetta, or Tess can be regarded both as sexual beings and 'pure women' - a contradiction which results in their surgical separation as body and soul. For the men there is a schematic good/bad division - Springrove as against Manston, Angel Clare as against Alex D'Urberville. Or, in *A Pair of Blue Eyes*, it is a more subtle distinction between simple love and unwilling love in Smith and Knight. These divisions may be traced back as early as 1866 in the split personae of 'The Two Men' which reflects Hardy's fundamental uncertainty as to what his motives were or who he was.

XXX - A FINAL PHASE

After July 1870 Hardy could only respond to the events of his cousin's life from a distance. Such effects may be plausibly traced at several junctures. Hardy's indifference to pushing ahead the publication of *Desperate Remedies* in the summer of 1870 is to be connected with his final interview with Tryphena in July 1870. The references of *An Indiscretion* make this clear enough. The dispatch of 'Destiny and a Blue Cloak', with its extraordinarily intimate references to Tryphena, just a week before his wedding suggests how ambiguous his feelings for Emma were from the very start of their marriage. Tryphena's own marriage to Charles Gale at Christmas 1877 may have been the cue for Hardy's attempt to write off the literary capital of *The Poor Man* in his novella *An Indiscretion* which was asked for in January 1878 and which he completed in June. Its first part follows the calendar of 1865, its second part, with detailed reference to *Desperate Remedies*, takes the story down to the time of the cousins' parting in 1870. It retains the original denouement of *The Poor Man* with the death of the heiress on the eve of her marriage. But the extensive plundering of the text of the lost novel - so many of its doublets can be located in *An Indiscretion* - suggest that this resource which had been associated with Tryphena from the first was one he no longer wished to husband.

After Tryphena's marriage her image temporarily disappears from view. In the costume drama *The Trumpet Major* not a vestige of it can be found. But it instantly returns with *A Laodicean* which opens with the twenty-five year old Somerset who has just thrown up architecture and is attended by sunset gnats. Variations on the story of 1865 are still clearly to be found in *The Mayor of Casterbridge* and *The Woodlanders*. But with Tryphena's death the story of 1865 once more comes to dominate Hardy's imagination. It is the theme that links the last three novels, despite their strong divergence of manner.

In giving *Tess* the structure of a 'duplicate 1865' Hardy resurrected the plan of *Desperate Remedies* and *A Pair of Blue Eyes*. The plan shows that Tryphena's inspiration is anything but incidental. She is present in the book from the moment Hardy conceived the ground-plan of the whole novel. Traces of the story of 1865 are carefully worked into the narrative - along with the sunset gnats. The retrospective insertion of the jewels episode and the thematic affinity of the

Stonehenge scene with 'The Revisitation' underline the identification with Tryphena at cardinal points of the narrative.

Given the ground-plan of the book there are probably other moments in the narrative where Hardy evoked reminiscences of his cousin. For instance, there is the dance at which Clare first sees Tess. It begins their story like the dance of *Under the Greenwood Tree* which appears to be a fictional transformation of Hardy's visit to the Sparks' house on Boxing Day 1864. There is Tess's intention to be a Pupil Teacher, a career only thinly veiled from the reader in her 'musical education' of Mrs. D'Urberville's birds. Not only does Tess bring the charges she has taught for examination by the mistress, but the whole episode, by way of Miss Gruchette - who, like Tess, looks after the fowl in *Ethelberta* - derives from a plot sketch which Hardy made in 1871 in which the young heroine was explicitly a school teacher. Of course, Tryphena is doubly implicated, both as teacher and keeper of birds - her sister Rebecca, who lived with the Gales at Topsham, complains of the 'dirty birdcages' in which Tryphena kept her pets. There is also Hardy's recreation of the Thermidorean weather of 1865 that accompanies Clare's courtship at Talbothays, just as the exceptional storm which drives the northern birds before it at Flintcomb-Ash has every appearance of describing the exceptional storm of 10 January 1866 when the *Times* reported flocks of birds 'in myriads' driven before the violent arctic weather from the north.

In manner *Tess* does not represent a radical departure from what Hardy had done before. There is, though, an intensification. In *Tess* Wessex is still in full bloom - its sensuousness enhances the underlying pathos implied in one of Hardy's working titles - 'Too late, Beloved!' This pathos may have an immediate source. Hardy began work on *Tess* in the autumn of 1888. In October 1888 Tryphena wrote to her Aunt Mary and her cousin Polly Antell in Puddletown of her alarming state of health - 'I have been very delicate lately....I suffer in my chest and from weak heart.' These are details which, in the way of families, we may presume were passed on to Hardy.[61] So the whole of Tess, whose ground-plan vouches for the fact that it was 'about Tryphena' from the very outset, would seem to have been written under the shadow of her failing health, until eventually - with perfect consistency - Hardy could retrace his steps and insert the jewels episode into his manuscript, with its allusion to the crush at the Jeunes', to commemorate the exact day of Tryphena's death. Till now Tryphena had been alive while Hardy fashioned the novels which in greater or less detail draw inspiration from his relationship with her. Now that she was dead he may have sensed that he had been writing the kind of book he would not be able to write again. In *Life* he calls *Tess* 'the beginning of the end of his career as a novelist.'[62]

---

[61] How easily may be guessed from the fact that the same Mary and Polly Antell were engaged as housekeepers at Max Gate (certainly in April 1891) during the Hardys' absence.

[62] Mrs. Bromell recalled her mother Tryphena's statement that the characters of Hardy's novels 'were all real people'. Was the possibility of such recognition a motive for writing - one which would obviously evaporate once Tryphena had died? Mary and Polly Antells's presence at Max Gate may suggest a certain leakage of information about the living

The Pursuit of the Well-Beloved was the first novel Hardy was free to plan after the March 1890 of Tryphena's death. Its ground-plan memorialises her even more comprehensively than *Tess* had done. The double nineteen-year span from Tryphena's birth to her parting with Hardy in July 1870 and from 1870 until her death provides the template on which the elaborate edifice of the whole book is built. *The Well-Beloved* also reveals the true bearings of the jewels episode and the Stonehenge scene in Tess by making their references so much more particular - both in the realism with which Hardy imitates the events of his own life in 1890 and in his detailed use of 'The Revisitation' for the finale of the novel.

But the bloom has withered. *The Well-Beloved* is an extraordinarily gaunt, schematic production projected by the bare outlines of its Portland setting. There is an unprecedented self-reflection in it, for the hero is for the first time an artist and one who is in some sense Hardy himself, as the allusions to his early verse and to the publication of *Desperate Remedies* make clear.

What is the meaning of this new development? It is almost as if Hardy could escape into a contemplation of Tryphena while she was still alive, but with her death he is cast back on himself. Tryphena is, of course, in the novel under cover of her various surrogates. But the fable's centre of gravity is closer to the figure of the artist and his 'inability to ossify with his generation.'

Tryphena, so that the novels might in one light be regarded as open wounds. Such an openness contrasts with the *closed* nature of the poems - not only as formal structures - but in the obsessive *antinomial* pattern, so patiently presented by Hynes, where the present closes off the past.

Inwardly he remains a young man through his infatuation with the well-beloved. But outwardly - almost with a touch of morbid satisfaction - Hardy seems to relish the disparity of Pierston's inevitable ageing when set beside the ever fresher renewals of the youthful Avice.[63] The macabre, even ludicrous state of being a 'young man of sixty' cannot be prolonged much further and since, in a professional way, the contemplations of a young man are the stuff of Hardy's novels the fable of *The Pursuit of the Well-Beloved* gives notice that his work as a novelist is all but over.

This meaning is made quite explicit in the 1897 revision of the book, but the narrative of the serial version already implies the destruction of the hero's art. The structural goal of *The Pursuit of the Well-Beloved* is Tryphena's death. Pierston's withering illness is contracted at the funeral of the second Avice - an Avice who is one of the cyclic reincarnations of Tryphena. Marcia appears at his bedside, her 'parchment-covered skull' borrowed from Tryphena's memorial poem 'The Revisitation', and as she passes before a photograph of the young Avice the Third - the latest of the cyclic reincarnations of Tryphena - 'The contrast of the aged Marcia's aspect, both with this portrait and with her

---

[63] In *Ethelberta* the cruel climax where the heroine finds herself carried off by her elderly lover was bodily transferred from the denouement of 'Destiny and a Blue Cloak' along with a number of details identifying Ethelberta with the Sparks family and - with her brows 'like a slur in music' - with Tryphena herself. *Jude* develops Sue Bridehead's feelings from the 1892 version of *The Well-Beloved* in the revulsion Avice III feels when her older husband enters her bedroom. In various ways all these heroines are linked with Tryphena and in relation to this January/May theme we cannot forget that Tryphena was eleven years Hardy's junior.

own fine former self, brought into his brain a sudden sense of the grotesqueness of things.' The awkward, indeed inexplicable expression 'both with this portrait and her own fine former self' is Hardy's note to himself that both Avice and Marcia are equally representatives of Tryphena and that Marcia's fine former self is therefore identical with the photograph of the youthful Avice. The identity is caught up in the punctuation of the succeeding sentence: 'His wife was - not Avice, but that parchment-covered skull moving about his room.' It is upon this composite picture of the youthful Tryphena that the ravaged emblem of the parchment-covered skull is such a grotesque superimposition. At this sight the narrative disintegrates with Pierston's hysterical cry, 'it is too, too droll - this ending to my would-be romantic history!'

The 1897 rewriting of the novel draws out the implication that the destruction of Pierston's would-be romantic history is synonymous with the destruction of his art. But even in the book's revised form there was a quality that its introverted fable - 'something light' for Tillotson's magazine - could never have contained. This was the monstrous, distorting anger that informs *Jude*. This anger is perhaps the aftermath of what had been a 'romantic history'. Now that the body and soul of Tess have been schematised into the carnal Arabella and the soulfully neurotic Sue there is no place for the romance which is the outward vesture of the Wessex Novels. Or - more pertinently - Hardy cannot now help seeing how equivocal that romance had always been.

The woman's sexuality is one thing that makes romance so equivocal. The difficulty hovers behind the portrait of Tess's protoype, Geraldine of *An Indiscretion*, who is described as a 'reckless though pure girl'. Or behind that of Lucetta in *The Mayor of Casterbridge* who protests 'that I was what I call innocent all the time they called me guilty.' Or, notoriously, with Tess in her provocative subtitle - 'A Pure Woman'. As early as the unpublished 'To a Bridegroom' of 1866 the girl's sexuality threatens to eclipse romance - 'Spread a tale that wronged her fame/Who'd not feel 'Of her enough!/Love is a foolish game?'' But Hardy can no longer hold these qualities in a synthesis. He must unpack them as 'The Body and Soul of Sue' - the sexual and a-sexual parts of the woman - and in so doing her romantic aura disintegrates. This, of course, is the inner explanation of why the death of the woman who is the second Avice or the parchment skull of Marcia robs the artist hero of *The Well-Beloved* of his power to create. Tryphena is a prose muse as long as her image can hold innocence and sexuality together. Her death, so far from enabling Hardy to idealise her, seems to have unlocked a final restraint which, retrospectively, shows how dominant the role of sexual sublimation had been in the existence of the young man.

This adjustment of vision is an inner change. With the disappearance of Tryphena as a focus of projection Hardy falls back on himself with a few frail shoots of self-examination. The title of this latest novel is well-chosen. Jude is not merely socially obscure, there is also an inner obscurity that Hardy makes some limited attempt to grapple with. Jude is the last in a long line of quasi-suicides stretching all the way back to young Swithin of *Two on a Tower*. Both Pierston of the serial version of *The Well-Beloved* and Jude commit thinly veiled suicides. Characteristically these heroes must lie down and expose themselves to the elements. The theme comes to prominence with Henchard's suicidal exposure which looks almost like an adult development of that vivid and troubling memory of Hardy's childhood when he lay on his back under his straw hat 'thinking how useless he was' and came to the conclusion that 'he did not want at all to be a man.' Pointedly Henchard crosses the scene of Hardy's childhood - Egdon Heath - to lay down his own unwanted life. Similarly the Jude who is about to expose himself to the elements crosses the field where he had scared birds as a child - the scene that ushers in that direct importation of the episode under the straw hat from the text of Hardy's autobiography. In death Jude murmurs the words of Job - 'Let the day perish wherein I was born, and the night in which it was said, There is a man child conceived.' Hardy has sedulously repeated the quotation from an earlier scene where Arabella writes to Jude from her London pothouse entrusting him with the unwanted Little Father Time.

This despair seems to have some sort of resonance in Hardy's childhood. Childhood - at the length it is treated in *Jude* - is an entirely new theme in the Wessex Novels and comparisons with *Life* show that in its essential chronological outline Hardy is recalling his own childhood here.

No attention has been paid to Hardy's discovery - when exactly we cannot say - that his mother had intended to leave him and escape from her marriage soon after his birth. This was her scheme of becoming a cook in a London club-house which only appears in all its poignancy in the typescript of *Life*. There, as Hardy notes, it was only 'the birth of children' - and this pathetic plural pointedly includes his younger sister Mary - that 'gave the death-blow to this rather adventurous scheme.' The fragile infant who was Hardy himself evidently did not count. It was such a precarious or conditional attachment to the mother which seems to inform Hardy's fundamental feeling of uselessness. In that key insight into his earliest self - the episode where the child reflects beneath his straw hat - Hardy introduces the reminiscence with the phrase 'thinking how useless he was'. When he transferred this reminiscence to the pages of *Jude* the phrase is replaced by the words, 'feeling more than ever his existence to be an undemanded one.' This is exactly the note struck when that intensified image of the unwanted child, Little Father Time, appears like nemesis - 'The poor child seems to be wanted by nobody!' This is Sue's verdict when the damaged child is dispatched to Jude in circumstances that seem suspiciously reminiscent of Jemima Hardy's club-house scheme - Arabella feels the child will be in the way now she is managing a London pothouse.

XXXI - A PORTRAIT OF A YOUNG GIRL

There is another childhood recorded in *Jude*. It is one that has very little thematic significance in the novel, but it may offer a key to the tragedy of Hardy's relations with his cousin. I refer to the childhood of Sue Bridehead, which is recalled in Aunt Drusilla's 'retrospective visions'.

Aunt Drusilla's reminiscences of Sue Bridehead form a very uncharacteristic little enclave of details. It is impossible to cite another instance from the novels in which Hardy describes a character's past in such a bundle of unrelated snippets. Aunt Drusilla recalls Sue wading in a pond at the age of twelve, 'her petticoats pulled above her knees' calling out, 'Move on, Aunty! This is no sight for modest eyes!' She recalls Sue's spirited participation in 'readings and renditions' arranged by the vicar. She recalls her sure sense of balance as she would 'hit in and steer down the long slide on yonder pond' to the admiration of the boys who would cheer her, when she would say, '"Don't be saucy, boys," and suddenly run indoors.' In the wake of these reminiscences Jude would like to look into the school where Sue's 'little figure had so glorified itself'. In isolation none of these reminiscences could be said to point decisively to Tryphena Sparks, but they are an ensemble and in this light a strong case can be made out for Tryphena as their original.

Sue's little figure had 'glorified' itself at school. Grace Melbury, whom Hardy identifies with Tryphena through his researches in Hutchins' *History*, is in one and the same sentence 'a flexible young creature' who is 'glorified' by her schooling. Sue takes part in readings and recitations, just as the first Avice does in *The Well-Beloved* - the Avice who is elaborately identified with Tryphena in the details of her death. I suspect a reference here to the evenings of readings and recitations inaugurated by the master of Puddletown School, Mr. Collins, in the first winter of Tryphena's tenure there as Pupil Teacher - readings which took place in the school, in which the pupils took part and which were hailed as a novelty by the Dorset County Chronicle.[64] Then Drusilla remembers how Sue could 'hit in and steer down the long slide on yonder pond' - a skill that may be paralleled with those feats of balance of Cytherea or Eustacia which are associated with that special 'gliding motion' which has every appearance of being an attribute of Tryphena.

Just as idiosyncratic is the reminiscence of Sue wading into a pond - a memory which can scarcely be dissociated from that discarded stanza still to be seen in the June 1868 draft of 'Retty's Phases' in which Retty recalls -

> that dear old day
> When you saw me wade
> Through the pond that people say
> Fairy shovels made.

The reference is highly specific, for the fairy shovels are a tradition about Rushy Pond, a short walk from the Bockhampton cottage.

The manuscript of 'Retty's Phases' - evidently a second draft of the poem[65] - is a most important document for the biographer. This stray notebook page

---

[64] Referring to the recitations Avice says, 'O but we are quite intellectual now. In the winter particularly.' The Puddletown readings were held monthly through the six winter months.
[65] See my article in *Thomas Hardy Society Review*, 1982, p.257.

is dated to 22 July 1868, less than a fortnight after Hardy completed fair-copying *The Poor Man*. The version of the poem that preceded this second manuscript draft was presumably written even nearer to the finish of the fair-copying of *The Poor Man*. That novel evidently had a calendar of 1865 and its heroine appears to have had both the features and the family circumstances of Tryphena Sparks. The novel had ended with the heroine's funeral, just as 'Retty's Phases' ends with the death and funeral of Retty. There seems to be a connection here that is not merely to be viewed in purely literary terms. For Hardy, as *Life* tells us in an exceptional admission, this was 'a time of mental depression'.

Once again we can rely on consistency. Not only does Retty seem to give us an early version of Sue's pond wading in *Jude* - it is such a specific event! - but she exhibits just the same sauciness that Sue shows on that occasion.

> Retty used to shake her head
> Look with wicked eye
> Say "I'd have you, idle Fred!
> If I cared to try"
> But she'd colour berry red
> Suddenly haste away
> Much afraid that things she'd said
> Were saucy things to say.

Just so Sue Bridehead says saucy things to her Aunt when she has her petticoats pulled above her knees or would say, '"Don't be saucy, boys," then suddenly run indoors.' There may be something of this temperament

- moderated by age - in Tryphena's ready retort to a member of the board appointing her to her Plymouth headship. He had a doubt about her youthfulness for the post. The twenty-year-old Tryphena countered with a smart, 'Well, sir, that is a thing that time will cure.' Even if the exchange is apocryphal it gives clear evidence of a reputation for the quick retort that Tryphena held in her family. She signs off a letter to her brother Nathaniel, 'How's your sweetheart old blow porridge Bibican.'

There are other hints in 'Retty's Phases'. Retty has some unspecified illness. The girl's illness is also an anxiety in the unpublished 1866 poem, 'To a Bridegroom'. Not only was Tryphena to die at the premature age of thirty-eight, but her health seems always to have been questionable. One of her interviewers for the Plymouth post writes that he has 'some doubt whether her physical strength is equal to the amount of exertion demanded' for a large school. In the 1866 'To a Bridegroom' there is also a clear hint of the provocative temperament in the words 'grew her love too wild to own'. But consistency seems to extend to even the tiniest details. So the physique of the young girl is defined in Sue Bridehead's 'little figure' and caught up in Retty's 'little body' and in the 'little fingers' of the girl of 'To a Bridegroom'.[66]

---

[66] If Sue's age of twelve, when she wades in the pond, is Tryphena's twelfth year this would give a date of 1863 which is quite consistent with the reference of the 1868 'Retty's Phases' to 'that dear old day'. The manuscript shows 'old' inserted into the line 'As I ran on that dear day' - the only extra-metrical word in the draft and one which seems dictated more by emotion than any poetic requirement.

Retty's experimental provocations touch on that 'unreserve' which is an inseparable component of the formula 'more of a woman in appearance than in years'. She can say 'I'd have you, idle Fred!' then suddenly run away, flushed with embarrassment. We can imagine such a taunt – and if Hardy blushed at a mere look from Louisa Harding he would certainly have blushed at this! – as the innocent grit that was to be developed into the tragic definition of Geraldine in *An Indiscretion* of whom the hero says 'she had certainly encouraged him' at the same time describing her as 'the reckless though pure girl' – and thus a prototype of the pure and passionate Tess whom Hardy identifies as his cousin Tryphena in the whole plan of her novel.

It can scarcely be said that these details owe their consistency to the fact that Hardy is merely sketching a temperament that intrigues him. The details are too idiosyncratic. Not only this, but all of them seem to relate to some aspect of that figure of Tryphena which enters Hardy's fictions as an external reality – a reality whose presence is betrayed by those anomalous details the fictions themselves cannot explain. These consistencies define a kernel which detaches itself sufficiently from its fictional contexts to give us some perception of how his cousin had struck Hardy as a young girl – a creature whose childish provocations sent out mixed messages, just as her prematurely developed physique caused her to 'be estimated as a woman when she was not much more than a child.' Given Hardy's recuperative state in the blazing Italian summer of 1865 these characteristics would seem to go a long way to explaining the disaster that ensued.

XXXII - FAREWELL TO THE NOVEL

Tess, like her predecessor Geraldine, is both an object of sensual attraction and 'A Pure Woman'. These are not, of course, altogether objective qualities - rather, they are how Hardy sees her. They are also qualities that are inside Hardy and which outline that conflict between his late-developing virility and that churchy youth whom Jemima hoped would live in chaste domesticity with his sister. In *Jude* such a dichotomy - which Hardy had originally located as 'The Body and Soul' of Tess - is projected into the contrasted figures of the carnal Arabella and the soulish Sue. But it is surely because this dichotomy maps out a conflict within Hardy himself that his own childhood comes to be such an important theme of the book, even if it is ultimately an incoherent one because Hardy cannot relate Jude's unwantedness as a child to his later difficulties with love. Jude, unlike his predecessor Pierston, now succeeds in taking his own life - the last in a line of quasi-suicides reaching back at least as far as *The Mayor of Casterbridge* and *Two on a Tower*. Mentally, we may feel, Hardy is poised over an abyss. No wonder he drew back and chose to tidy up *The Pursuit of the Well-Beloved*, rewriting its finale as an explicit farewell to the novel. 'Chose' is probably the wrong word, though. The revised finale of the book makes it clear that the inspiration of the artist who is both Pierston and Hardy has been destroyed by the death of a woman in 1890.

The 1897 revision retains the emblematic death of Tryphena as its narrative goal, but the ending of the book is now expanded to show Pierston coming to terms with his bereavement. The most notable change in this artist hero is the fact that 'the artistic sense had left him'. Pierston is no longer a creator. Just here the equation between Pierston the artist and Hardy the artist becomes concrete. It was already immanent in Pierston's verse writing and in his becoming A.R.A. Becoming A.R.A. was a gloss on Hardy's first appearance as a novelist with *Desperate Remedies*. Accordingly the revised version of *The Well-Beloved* is signed off with the notice that Pierston's name 'figured on the retired list of Academicians.' Hardy was as good as his word - he did not write another novel. Pierston's illness is emblematic of Hardy's response to his cousin's death. When the narrative directly attributes its artist hero's loss of creative power to this illness, we gather that Hardy is not only making a Prospero-like announcement of his retirement from the novel but giving a personal explanation for it in the bereavement which is the goal of the whole structure of the novel.

XXXIII - A NAPOLEONIC TONIC

Retrospectively the special meaning Hardy gives to the phrase *young man* becomes clear. It has its biographical aspect - Hardy is a young man from the moment he has intercourse with his cousin at the age of five-and-twenty to the time of her death when he is 'nearly fifty'. The 1897 revision of *The Pursuit of the Well-Beloved* not only sees Pierston's loss of artistic inspiration - it sees him suddenly age. The personal and the artistic are inextricably linked - in some sense Hardy's work as a novelist is the real inner existence of the young man. It is an existence carried on at Hardy's work-desk - an existence of creation and of day-dreams and regrets. The death of Tryphena rudely opens this world to reality once more. Of the emblematic illness which brings about his loss of artistic productivity Pierston says - 'That fever has killed a faculty which has, after all, brought me my greatest sorrows, if a few little pleasures.' In statements of such modest realism we see the whole venture of the Wessex Novels begin to crumble.

In the seven years between Tryphena's death and the 1897 revision of *The Well-Beloved* Hardy's remorse blows itself out. Traces of the story of 1865 are to be found in later poems, but it is surprising how few and sporadic these are. Immediately there seem to be a few references. The poem 'Her Immortality' is probably one. Its reference to the seven years that have elapsed since the death of the woman and its inclusion in the Wessex Poems of 1898 suggest a date of 1897. The poem itself dramatises the transition from violent despair to a measure of acceptance of the woman's death which parallels the establishment of a sort of calm in the rewritten finale of the 1897 *The Well-Beloved*. 'In Tenebris I', if it was also written in the 1895-6 of its two companion pieces, probably tells the same story, in particular its opening lines which with their collocation of 'Wintertime nighs' and 'bereavement pain' look suspiciously like an adumbration of Hardy's ceasing to be a young man at the death of Tryphena. Soon, with *The Dynasts*, Hardy escapes into the never-never land of the Napoleonic Wars, just as he had in 1868 at the time of his 'mental depression' with an outline of a poem on the Battle of the Nile, or after Tryphena's marriage to Charles Gale with the costume drama of *The Trumpet-Major*.

XXXIV - THE MUSE

This brief sketch of the evidence for Tryphena's place in Hardy's life and art implies an important place. I am not sure that I have managed to resolve the bugbear or syzygy of literary biography - those awkward bedfellows art and life. Personally my interest has been to illuminate the life, rather than interpret the works in the light of any biographical discovery. If I have made a case for drawing a biographical implication from fictions - those calendars again! - I suppose those fictions must now read slightly differently. But I think of that difference as an added layer rather than a radical alteration of our impressions as innocent readers. I have tried to keep in mind the difficulty that such 'documentary' elements as I find in the fictions instantly shade off into fiction proper. That is a difficulty, but it scarcely justifies the riposte of denying a reality to such elements in the name of some absolute aesthetic purity. Any literary biography sets its stall out on grounds of impurity - in the background the works are always supplying an illicit interest to what might otherwise have seemed a dull enough life. For us the implication may be that an author is most alive at his desk, when - for the biographer - he has no life at all. At least I can say that some of the 'documentary' elements I have pointed to enable us to look over Hardy's shoulder as he works and glean some vague idea of the life-issues that inspired or perhaps distracted him as he wrote. If I wanted to be a little sententious I could call this a phenomenological view of Thomas Hardy.

Tryphena is not, of course, Hardy's only literary woman. There is Emma Gifford. But even here the role of Hardy's first wife must be modified. A poem like 'The Voice of Things' clearly does not belong to her and at the same time shows that the seascape of remorse was already a form in Hardy's mind before Emma had died and before he could embark on the Poems of 1912-13. Much earlier it is also clear that Emma has only a superficial place in *A Pair of Blue Eyes* and I use the word advisedly to draw attention to surface appearance. At the level of its ground-plan this novel, like *Desperate Remedies* and a number of its greatest successors, is a book of 1865 and therefore a book that is in some sense 'about Tryphena'. With a characteristic blend of literalism and evasion Hardy qualifies Emma's importance by telling us the plot of the novel was 'one that he had thought of and written down long before he knew her.' Hardy may be attracted to the stories of other women he had known. Elizabeth-Jane in *The Mayor of Casterbridge* may, as Millgate suggests, have been inspired as a sort of composite of Eliza and Jane Nicholls. But I cannot concede that Tryphena is one among many or even that she is *prima inter pares*.

Tryphena has a role in Hardy's authorship of quite a different order of significance. She is the initiator. Of Hardy's juvenile verse we have only 'Domicilium'. Though the poem has a distinct atmosphere it is one that owes too much to Wordsworth. But the poems of

1865-7, dominated as they must once have been by the maiden of the complete cycle of 'She, to Him' sonnets, are suddenly Hardy. They show a weight and power characteristic of some of his much later verse. As the maiden of the sonnets it is difficult to deny Tryphena her crucial influence on this beginning.

The Poor Man is only further evidence of that transition from would-be author to a writer of real power. The feeble sketch 'How I built Myself a House', written at the end of 1864 and published early in the following year, shows the wish rather than the ability to become an author. Two years later, in those doublet passages we can recover from *The Poor Man*, we find the Hardy of delicate originality and real descriptive power. *Under the Greenwood Tree* preserves one of those doublets - shared with *An Indiscretion* - which shows the young teacher Fancy Day with Tryphena's precise features and also her 'speciality' of gliding motion. We may take it then that Tryphena was both the heroine and the inspiration of *The Poor Man* as she had been the inspiration of the poems of 1865-7. The word inspiration must be used intuitively, since it is impossible to quantify, but there is here some sort of pointer to the human realities behind Hardy's sudden emergence as a writer.

Tryphena's image continues to hover at the back of the Wessex Novels. *The Poor Man* and many of the subsequent novels cover the same autobiographical ground that the poems of 1865-7 had sketched out. In pointing to the recurrence of the calendar for 1865 even in novels as late as *Tess* and *The Well-Beloved* it is clear that the story of that year continued to feed Hardy's imagination. But the most powerful evidence for Tryphena's importance seems to lie in Hardy's motives for ceasing to be a novelist. He may have felt bruised by the reception of his late manner, but this is a sensitivity which may be somewhat discounted in the fact that the journal note on the germ of *Jude the Obscure* already had a belligerence that seems set to court such a reaction. Hardy's innermost explanation seems to be found in the analysis made by *The Well-Beloved* where Pierston's loss of inspiration and retirement as academician stem from the illness contracted at the funeral of one of the recurring representatives of Tryphena.

Exploration of the role of the calendar of 1865 in the plotting of the novels suggests that Tryphena is anything but an incidental inspiration. It is her image which unfolds the plans of the earliest and some of the latest of these great edifices. We can see 1865 as a template which informs the broad outlines of these books as well as many intimate details of the characterisation of their heroines. Of course, Hardy had always wanted to be an author and in his novels we cannot say exactly which things - let alone that everything is 'about Tryphena'. But his cousin is the key that first turned desire into reality. Without Tryphena it is just possible that Hardy would have become the poet we recognise, but certainly not the novelist.

The price this authorship demanded was rejection. Tryphena is one of a roll-call of Hardy's rejected women - Lousia Harding, Eliza Nicholls, Cassie Pole - Emma Hardy herself. Through the thickets of a reconstruction it is difficult to say why Tryphena occupied a special place in such a list. Partly it may be the guilt of Hardy's connection with her as the young girl she was in 1865. Partly it may be that she inaugurated his *young manhood* in a sexual sense. Partly it may be surprise - that the child he had always known should be transformed into an object of sexual desire. Depression had broken a way through his habitual repression - from being familiar with Tryphena as infant and child he was, we may suppose, surprised into such an affair. He was temporarily stripped of those bookish defences which he was so prompt to re-erect in the form of a sonnet-cycle and the other miscellaneous poems of 1865-7. For a brief moment he had been without such a defence. There is a beautiful and uncharacteristic passage in *An Indiscretion*. Up to a certain moment the affection of the two principals 'had been a battle, a species of antagonism wherein his heart and the girl's had faced each other....But now it was a truce and a settlement, in which each one took up the other's utmost weakness, and was careless of concealing his and her own.' Somehow authorship is sparked by this receding vision of authenticity. I have reviewed those hints that Hardy's family kept him abreast of the outlines of his cousin's domestic achievement - her work, her marriage and her children. Such humanity must have been a constant and uncomfortable foil to his talent.

APPENDIX - THE 'RARE DEVICE'

The naming of Cytherea Graye by way of Gray's *Progress of Poesy* shows a complexity of reference at work behind the scenes from the time of Hardy's first published novel. But such a cast of mind is already evident in the poems as early as 1867 in the 'rare device/Of reds and purples' which makes a fleeting appearance in 'Heiress and Architect'.

Purple has something to do with Tryphena. 'In a Eweleaze Near Weatherbury' supplied 'The Revisitation' with the curious rhyme of chisel/grizzel, but its 'blazon of my prime' may also have been the cue for the opening stanza of 'The Revisitation' with its 'hopes that heralded each seeming brave and bright time/Of my primal purple years.' Purple primal years, in the light of the biographical bearings of the poem, might be glossed - the time of my association with Tryphena before July 1870. Equally clearly it is Tryphena who is invested with the 'bloom of young Desire, and purple light of Love', borrowed from the poet Gray, in her guise as the dancing Cytherea Graye who appears as a young girl at mixed Christmas parties. Similarly Gray's purple light is explicitly applied to Grace Melbury and in the revised version of *The Well-Beloved* the 'majestic bloom' given to Marcia at the close of the tale is no doubt indebted to Gray as well. Both these heroines are given specific characterisations which link them with Tryphena.

But the 'rare device / Of reds and purples' does not really make sense until we do what Hardy must have done and turn up the Greek lexicon for the nearest homophones to *Phena*. Tryphena was familiarly known in her family as Triffie, but Phena is what Hardy calls his cousin in the one poem he explicitly connects with her. Phena is also the name of a bird in Tess's charge - an invention that can date from no more than a year or so prior to the writing of 'Thoughts of Phena'. In his lexicon the words that specially drew Hardy's attention were *phene*, *phoenix* and *phoenicopterus*.

Phoenix is a colour word which Hardy could find in his Liddell and Scott glossed as 'a purple-red, deep purple or crimson', so that our suspicions may be aroused by a 'rare device / Of reds and purples'.[67]

Phene is glossed in the lexicon as 'a kind of vulture'. In 'The Wind's Prophecy' we find 'the headland, vulturine.' Hardy describes this poem as 'Rewritten from an old copy' and there is reason to date the original from at least as early as 1867. The poem has breakers which 'Huzza like a mad multitude'.[68] This was an image which found its way into the much later poem 'The Voice of Things' where 'The waves huzza'd like a multitude below'. But the words had already made an appearance in *Ethelberta*, where there are 'waves sending up a sound like the huzzas of multitudes' and here they occur in a matrix of details

---

[67] Phoenix is also the legendary bird and this may be why Hardy calls the reincarnated heroines of *The Well-Beloved* Avice - like Latin avis, a bird. In *Life* Hardy gives the alternative spellings 'Avis or Avice'. When Pierston describes of the migration of his Well-Beloved, he sees her 'turn from flame to ashes, from a radiant vitality to a corpse....Each mournful emptied shape stands ever after like the nest of some beautiful bird from which the inhabitant has departed...'

[68] The cryptic line which precedes it - 'The waves outside where breakers are' - might be accounted for by the Portland breakwater.

shared with *The Well-Beloved*. These parallelisms between the novels may be most readily explained by a common origin in *The Poor Man* of 1867 suggesting a date in this year or some time prior to this year for the original version of 'The Wind's Prophecy'. But the headland of 'The Wind's Prophecy' seems always to have been Portland - 'the headland, vulturine / Snores like old Skrymer in his sleep'. At the opening of *The Well-Beloved* Portland is described as 'the head of a bird' which has both its 'afternoon sleep' and its 'snores'.

The unexceptionable 'head of a bird' is an emendation of the 1897 version of *The Well-Beloved*. It replaces the truly weird characterisation of Portland as 'the head of a flamingo' in the 1892 serial version. In the lexicon 'flamingo' glosses the Greek word *phoenicopterus*. Hardy's choice of the equally bizarre alternatives of vulture and flamingo - neither of them Dorset birds! - to characterise Portland only finds an explanation in his researches in Liddell and Scott. If the 'jutting height / Coloured purple' of 'The Place on the Map' is also Portland we would have a triple confirmation of this arcane conceit - a Portland which is *phene* and *phoenicopterus* and now, in the colour purple, *phoenix* as well.

But the first two of these form a quite sufficient conjunction to gloss the 'rare device / Of reds and purples' as *phoenix* the colour-word and to see that Hardy was more than justified in calling his discovery a 'rare device'. 'Heiress and Architect', in which the phrase 'rare device' occurs, dates from 1867 and so in all likelihood does the vulturine headland of 'The Wind's Prophecy'.

The conceit Phena/phoenix is a key which unlocks much later poems such as 'Alike and Unlike'. In May 1893 Hardy recorded the 'Magnificent deep purple-grey mountains' which he and Emma saw near Llandudno. The MS. of 'Alike and Unlike' has the significant indication 'She speaks', so that it is an Emma who now realises the very different meaning the purples had had for Hardy and for herself when they had both originally seen them on their way to Llandudno. She now realises that the scene had superimposed on it 'Gravings on your side deep, but slight on mine.' The pun is both an engraved line and a grave - for Hardy the deep grave of Tryphena who had died three years before and for Emma the slighter (to Hardy's mind) grave of her recalcitrant father, who had died some months after Tryphena. For Hardy the 'purple-grey' of his journal note has been split into the purple which stands for Tryphena and the 'tragic, gruesome, gray' of his grief at her death or at a life which no longer contains her existence. The symbolism and - most pointedly - Emma's exclusion from it is handled with precisely the same significance in the funereal re-colouring of the Cornish coast in Hardy's Preface to *A Pair of Blue Eyes* of March 1895. Here the cliffs' 'bloom of dark purple cast' picks up Liddel and Scott's definition of *phoenix* as 'deep purple', just as the mountains behind Llandudno are 'deep purple-grey'. But as the Preface asserts this is only a perception 'for one person' so that Emma is again pointedly excluded.

The lexicon may also accommodate gray in the colour word *glaukos*, glossed as 'pale green, bluish-green, gray...' In *A Pair of Blue Eyes* Elfride's entry into the church causes Stephen Smith's world 'to be lit by 'the purple light' in all its definiteness'. Hardy is continuing the symbolism drawn from Gray's *Progress of Poesy*. The equation grey=Gray may have distracted him, but his sharp eye could scarcely miss the intersection of 'blue-eyed Pleasures', in the brief strophe of the *Progress of Poesy* where he had discovered his purple bloom, with the lexicon's definition of glaukos as 'of the eye, light blue or gray' which would seem to have supplied the title of the novel. *Glaukos* also supplies the 'bloom' of the Hambro' grape in the climactic description of the Cliff without a Name in chapter twenty-one, since *glaukos* is also the greyish green or blue bloom of the grape. By these means Hardy seems to have ingeniously united both the bloom and the purple of Gray's 'bloom of young Desire, and purple light of Love'. So we are told with Hardy's egregious italics that Elfride's lips 'were red, *without* the polish cherries have' so that Knight can later kiss them 'with the carefulness of a fruiterer touching a bunch of grapes so as not to disturb their bloom.' *A Pair of Blue Eyes* is saturated with this colour symbolism. A characteristic instance is the opening paragraph of chapter five where the 'warm tone of light from the fire' (the lexicon also glosses phoenix as 'the colour of fire'[69]) is made to contrast with a medley of 'grayish' tones. The trees and grass are a 'grayish-green', just as Stephen sees 'monotonous gray-green grass'

---

[69] q.v. '...you could fancy the colour of Eustacia's soul to be flame-like. The sparks from it that rose into her dark pupils gave the same impression.'

from his window at the Rectory. In chapter twenty these have become 'neutral green hills'.

Hardy began work on *A Pair of Blue Eyes* in the summer of 1871, but the glaucous symbolism may already occur in the emphatic grays of the 1867 poem 'Neutral Tones' to which the very title draws attention. The first stanza concludes with the leaves - 'They had fallen from an ash, and were gray.' The last stanza ends with 'a pond edged with grayish leaves.' Hardy has surely got this 'grayish' colour from the lexicon where *glaukos* is the greyish-green 'of the olive, of the willow, and also of the vine'. The conceit dates from the same year as the 'rare device/Of reds and purples' in 'Heiress and Architect' when the complex naming of Cytherea Graye with the start of work on *Desperate Remedies* is only two years in the future.